Incidents Beyond Coincidence

by
Dolora Cook Deal
and
Winston H. Cook

May, 2003

First edition

WynLora Publishing   Hope, Idaho

Incidents Beyond Coincidence
By Dolora Cook Deal and Winston H. Cook

Published by

WynLora publishing
900 Trestle Creek Road
Hope, Idaho 83836

ISBN 0-9740477-0-8

First Printing May 2003
Second Printing August 2003

Printed in the United States of America
By
Copy-Rite Printing
Spokane, Washington

Cover Art

The cover art was created by a young college student, Adam Bohrer. Adam as a youngster had and retains the ability to see Angels. When Adam was ten I asked him if he could see my angel. His response was, "yes." He said, " It has a beautiful multi-colored skirt made out of flower petals." I asked him how to see angels and he explained, "You have to look with a different part of your eye, the back part." When my brother and I started to create this book I asked Adam if he remembered what my angel looked like and could he use his computer program to design a book cover. Adam complied with my request in exchange for a double batch of chocolate chip cookies every month to be sent where he is a student at the American University in Paris. Adam, thank you so much for not getting bogged down in the limitations and boundaries of the everyday mind.

Love Dolora

Table of Contents

Page

Contact   1
Dolora-Experiencing the peace that passes understanding

"Lord take me from this, this is more than I can stand."   13
Winston-On fire from the waist up, I have an out of body
experience

The Voice Within

Hypothermia, a Peaceful Way to Die   31
Winston-My first experience with voices in my head

The Burgundy Jaguar   35
Winston-A wistful question is immediately answered in my head

Requests for Divine Help

Courage To Fly   41
Dolora-Age is relative

207 Sunrise   47
Dolora-Sometimes you have to get angry

Direct Petition   51
Winston-I want to do the wrong thing, but I ask for help

The Phantom Road Grader   63
Dolora-Clearing the road less traveled

The Valley of the Shadow

Drowning   69
Dolora-Faith at five, not afraid to die

Slashing Clear-cuts   73
  Winston-Daily close calls

Hit by a Tree   77
  Winston-A logging accident has long-lasting positive results

Trial by Fire   83
  Dolora-Uncle Cliff saves my dog, my house and my life

Asleep at the Wheel   87
  Winston-I drive off the road

Bashed by a Buick   91
  Winston-I am hit by a car while on my bicycle

Broadway Exit   99
  Dolora-Driven to exhaustion

Feathers, Fur, and Nature

Papers and Protection   107
  Dolora-Surrounded by furry love

Scraggles   111
  Winston-An animal metaphor for life

Ryan's Black Baron   115
  Dolora-A doggie comedian moves on

Angels in the Orchard   121
  Winston-Apricots saved from a killer frost

Bubba   125
  Dolora-Chocolate is good for everyone

Findhorn/Perelandra Experiment   129
  Winston-A winter garden in Washington

The Crying Tree   133
  Dolora-Why do trees cry?

The Dove   137
  Dolora-Asking for a sign and receiving it

A Rock with a Hole In It   141
  Dolora-How to find one

Walking with Donner   145
  Dolora-The social director of the bike path

Perfect Timing

One-lane Bridge   151
  Winston-Two vehicles pass in the night

Connecting with a Mentor   155
  Winston-A persistent teacher changes my life

V.D.   161
  Dolora-Venereal Disease or validating a life

The Warm Letter   165
  Winston-Reassurance of the future

The House that Blew Down   169
  Winston-A man is killed, three are injured, in a house I was
  supposed to be in

Angela   173
  Dolora-Why am I here?

No One Cares 177
 Dolora-Healing the World

In the Flow 181
 Winston-A weekend of effortless accomplishment, a model

Last Goodbyes 191
 Dolora-Farewell to my father

Gay 195
 Dolora-Choosing between heart and head, heart wins

Visions and Dreams

A Golden Vision 201
 Winston-A future blessed with success and prosperity

Finding a New Wife 205
 Winston-A second time around

Messages from Beyond

Rosamond 215
 Dolora-Love is forever, a message from the other side

Just Listen 219
 Dolora-A message from the other side

"Everything is Just Fine Here, Sis" 223
 Winston-A message from the other side

"Just Love Everything" 229
 Winston-A message from the other side

"Roses for Emily" 231
 Dolora-A message from the other side

Forward

We have shared our lives as brother and sister. This book is an attempt to witness the love, protection, blessings, and divine interventions that have occurred and are ongoing in our lives. The first two stories became the foundation for the subsequent life-changing experiences. The initial experiences were intense enough to cause us to examine our lives before and after the event and record the many other times we have been touched, taught, guided, and saved from harm.

None of the other stories are as dramatic as the first two, but as a whole they establish a pattern of constant, caring, love. We feel these types of events happen to many people but are dismissed as luck or coincidence. This book is a documentation of our perceptions of actual events that have happened to us. We have purposefully tried not to interpret and apply labels regarding what or who is responsible for these incidents, and let readers come to their own conclusions.

As you read these stories, we hope you will reflect on the Incidences Beyond Coincidences that you have experienced.

Dolora and Winston

Contact
By Dolora

I was thirty-five and standing at the door to a very cool and sterile private room in a Seattle Hospital. It was hot and humid outside. The July sun was shining down across Puget Sound, creating an image of tranquility. I had just taken the ferry from Winslow on Bainbridge Island to downtown Seattle. I was about to undergo surgery to have a hysterectomy and I was pregnant with my third child. I didn't know if I was doing the right thing. Something inside me kept prompting me to ask myself the question, "Am I making the correct decision?" I had undergone a partial hysterectomy at age twenty-seven due to severe endometriosis. My first child, a beautiful baby girl born in 1972, was a fertility-pill baby. When she was born, the mother instinct in me was so strong that I felt I would truly rip apart anybody with my teeth if they tried to harm my child. Three years later I became pregnant a second time with no fertility drugs and we had a perfect baby boy. Both children were wonderful and healthy. I felt truly blessed to be a mother.

I had graduated from college with a degree in medical technology, but in truth all I ever wanted to be was a wife and mother. Having a home of my own and being the best parent I could be was the only goal I had ever pictured in my mind. I had no aspirations of setting the world on fire with my brilliance or beauty, I just wanted a happy, loving family and a husband who could understand and accept me, in other words, love me as I am.

When I became pregnant a third time, while using birth control, and with only part of one ovary, I was astounded. I knew something was terribly wrong with my body. I had realized I was pregnant within about three days after intercourse. My breasts had gone through changes and were sore. My abdomen cramped constantly, which was not a typical pregnancy for me. Normally, once I became pregnant, the rest was easy. This was very different. The doctor told me I was going to miscarry and that I would have to have surgery within a year because all my endometriosis had returned.

It made no sense to me to wait until I miscarried to have surgery. I knew my body had been seriously damaged by the endometriosis before I'd had my first surgery. I didn't want to do that again. I was hurting constantly. Fear of surgery was not an issue; I had worked in a hospital for several years as a medical technologist and I knew I could deal with the pain.

What I didn't understand was why I was pregnant a third time. I felt that God must have some special mission for me. Maybe I was destined to have a child with problems in order to receive growth. After all, the chances that I could become pregnant while using birth control and with only part of one ovary were pretty slim. Well, God certainly had my attention if that was his intention. I prayed constantly to know his will.

I had been meditating for an hour every morning for three years while Sesame Street aired on PBS. I could set my children in front of the TV and grab a whole hour for myself uninterrupted. My meditation consisted of relaxing myself, taking several deep breaths, and visualizing white light coming into my body. I had never had any instruction in meditation, but my mom had said, "Send love to all those you care about."

Well, I had no clue about how to generate the feeling of love in my body so I could send it out, but I knew I always felt unconditional love when I was in the presence of my best friend Sharon.

So I thought of Sharon and filled myself with that feeling of unconditional love and started thinking of everyone I knew in the United States. I started in the state of Washington and preceded across the whole US and Canada. Then I thought of everyone I knew in Europe, and then I covered every continent with my love. I ended my meditation by visualizing everyone in the world holding hands around the equator directing love to the earth. When I first started meditating it only took about fifteen to twenty minutes, but after three years it was taking me at least an hour to send love to everyone. I grew to treasure this quiet time by myself. It was no longer an effort but a joy. In three years I never missed a day of sending love.

However, now I was in a difficult situation. My

husband, Steve, was very concerned, and every time he looked at me he would cry. I really needed some emotional support and I wasn't sure what God wanted of me. I sent Steve home to be with the children and I started to pray. For some reason the nurses had not given me any medication to relax me. I have never done drugs of any kind except a little wine now and then. It was evening, supper was served, but I wasn't allowed to eat because of the upcoming surgery. I was not feeling deprived because I remembered my first surgery, when I had vomited for days afterward.

Just then a beautiful lady in a long white gown came into my room. I remember looking at her dress and seeing no seams in it, but somehow that did not seem at all unusual, even to an experienced home seamstress, which I was. The lady's hair was silver and shimmering. She must have been about six feet tall. She explained to me that she was the wife of one of the hospital board members, and that seemed like a reasonable explanation for her visit. We started discussing my situation and she gave me great comfort, assuring me I was doing the right thing. We talked for three hours. Not once did a nurse come in to interrupt us. I fell asleep saying to God, "If I'm not supposed to have this surgery, let me know and I will get up and walk out of this room." God didn't say anything that I could translate as an answer. I fell into a fitful sleep praying for guidance.

The nurses came to take me to surgery early the next

morning. I still had been given no medication of any kind. When I arrived in the operating room I asked the anesthesiologist if he wanted me to move myself onto the surgery table. He said, "This one is still awake. What shall we do with it?" I was given an injection and the surgery proceeded as planned. I woke up later with my husband telling me to breathe deeply. He was great. His continual verbal reminder to keep breathing deeply as I slipped in and out of consciousness helped me clear the anesthesia quickly. I was up the very next day.

I asked the nurses about the lady who had stayed in my room for three hours, but no one seemed to know anything about her. One nurse said she had seen her, but knew nothing else. I had wanted to thank her for the incredible comfort and compassion she had given me.

I was in the hospital for only a couple of days and I was anxious to get home to my babies. Steve and the children came to retrieve me. My body was sore and aching. The ferry ride was the quickest way home, but it was almost more than I could handle. Many friends came to visit, one of them with a cold, and I caught a cold that developed into pneumonia. I thought I would die every time I coughed or laughed. My body healed in a timely manner and I was back to my old routine in about six weeks. But my emotions were a mess. I didn't know if I was a he, a she, or why had the anesthesiologist had said, "What shall we do with IT?" The doctor had put me on estrogen since I had no ovaries.

Hot flashes coursed through me regularly, but not too badly. It's just that I had just lost my whole identity. I knew I would never become pregnant again; I would never nurse another baby. I loved nursing my babies. I wasn't sure what role I was to play in society, even in my family. In Native American Spirituality they say that when a woman can no longer bear children she becomes a crone. I didn't want to think of myself as a crone. The connotation was certainly not very sexy or appealing, and I was only thirty-five. I was seeking balance but I didn't know where to find it. I started flirting with a male friend who was younger than I just to see if I could still attract a man. He became interested in me and wanted to have an affair. Part of me, the ego part, wanted the excitement and attention that having an affair would give me. The other part knew how destructive it could be, and most of all I wanted to keep my family intact.

I was fighting with my ego all the time. I needed to know I was still an attractive female. I was not an IT. I was torn between the excitement of being desired, and keeping my children in an intact family environment. This friend would call me on a regular basis and ask to meet me somewhere. I didn't know how to battle that part of me that needed assurance of my desirability.

One night, after I put the children to bed, I went down to the basement to sew. Sewing had always been a source of solace to me. But I sat there for a while and then I started praying, "God, help me. Why can't I be content with who I am and what I have?" In an instant I was filled with peace, the most amazing peace I have ever felt. It surrounded me, and then a voice started to speak very clearly. The voice came from above me and over my right shoulder. The voice said, "Dolora, you have never wanted the same thing with your body that you wanted with your soul. I'll show you the way." The voice spoke to me as clearly and naturally as a best friend might talk to you in absolute confidence.

In the Bible you read about the peace that passes all understanding and for the first time in my life I felt unconditional love. The longing inside of me that had always been searching for that unknown something was now quiet. I found it difficult to believe that God was talking to me, but what else could it be? I had heard the words and no one was visibly there. The words had been very clear. "I can do nothing further with you spiritually until you unite your body and soul, I'll show you the way."

I was amazed at the peace I felt. My whole life had changed in an instant. I no longer desired the attention of men to give me worth; God was talking to me! I had been seeking this kind of feeling all of my life. The only way I can describe it is to say that suddenly I was quiet inside, there was nothing driving me to be more, to have more. This was true peace and it was a unique and new feeling. To this day I have never felt anything as beautiful as that first connection to the spirit of Jesus, God,

Buddha, The Great White Father, or whatever label you chose to put on the energy that pervades all of life.

The next day, when my male friend called, I asked him not to call me again because I had arrived at a place in my life where I had always wanted to be, emotionally and spiritually. He honored my request and ceased to call.

This overwhelming love permeated every aspect of my life. As I walked I was surrounded by peace. In one night I had been reborn. I listened constantly for the voice to speak to me again. My physical life started changing rapidly. Pan Am, the company employing my husband, encouraged couples to take a Human Effectiveness Course being offered by the United Learning Institute in Tacoma. Pan Am even paid the five-hundred-dollar price tag for couples who signed up to take the course. This class taught me to take responsibility for everything that was in my life. I came to understand that whatever happened to me, I either allowed the circumstances or created them. I was free to accept or change anything and everything. I was no longer a victim of my emotions.

I didn't hear this voice again for another seven years, but the peace remained with me and that was enough. I never lost the feeling of being loved by some special force. I continued to grow and take responsibility for all that I was. Some of what I was, wasn't very pretty, but I had to learn to love myself as God loved me.

I was seeking truth with every fiber of my being. I meditated, explored metaphysical experiences, had a past life regression, and went to a workshop to connect with my guardian angel sponsored by the Unity Church. Each of these experiences inspired profound growth in my life.

My past life regression explained to me the relationships in my current life. They finally all made sense. In the angel workshop we journeyed through a guided meditation to the time before we were born to find our purpose in life. I saw my purpose in blazing letters written on a beautiful wooden table. I was to become a BEACON OF TRUTH according to the message my ego saw. In reality, I was simply to BECOME THE TRUTH of my being. My ego really wanted to be the center of the big picture.

At forty-two years of age, I again heard the voice. The communication lasted for fifteen hours and I got to have a two-way dialogue, asking questions, hearing answers and being surrounded by the incredible feeling of unconditional love and peace. I had been seeking truth in every corner and my search had led me to look at those things I fear. When fear lives in your body, that part of your body cannot vibrate in love and trust. I had become terrified of a person I had met. I found out later that this person was into witchcraft but I did not know it at the time, thank God.

I was terrified of the "dark side" and when I discovered this person could read my mind, without my permission, I became paranoid. I didn't have any idea how to protect myself from this woman. I couldn't sleep I couldn't eat. I was praying constantly, asking for answers. I told my husband we had to get out of town. He indulged my paranoia; we took the children, and headed on a ski trip to Canada. I was trying to hide my distress from the children, but inside I was screaming in fear. My husband and the children went to look for some skis for our daughter and I stayed in the car. I was in such a state of fear that I said, "God, I can't live this way any longer, it's been a week of sheer terror. You must take my life or take my fear."

Suddenly, the peace flowed over me again. I felt the presence again. My family was headed for Grouse Mountain outside of Vancouver, B.C., to ski. I could finally breathe. Skis in hand we all loaded on the tram. I stood there looking out the windows, grateful to be released from the fear. I was paying no attention to the people getting on the tram as Steve asked me, "How many people do you think are on this tram?" I was still looking out the window as I answered without pausing, "There are seventy-nine people here." The digital counter in the tram flashed seventy-nine just after that comment. I had not even been aware that there was a counter. Steve questioned, "How did you know that?" As we started skiing down the mountain the voice started asking me questions. I would answer them. All the questions related to the amount of control I was willing to release in my current life. I then asked the voice, "What is God?"

The reply, "I am the life force within, nothing less, nothing more. I am the life force in everything." I then asked, "Why are we here, what is the purpose of life?" The voice replied, "life is a gift, the purpose is JOY."

The internal dialogue continued as I skied down the mountain. It was late afternoon the children were hungry. We headed out to have dinner at Earl's, a wonderful restaurant in Vancouver. It was the first time I'd been able to eat in a week, and everything tasted alive and delicious. I was exhausted, but the voice kept asking me questions about how much was I willing to trust the God force within to direct my life. Could I release all the things my ego had attachment to? I asked if I could sleep and continue in the morning. The voice said, "Yes, sleep in peace, my child."

This all happened long before *Conversations With God* became a household word. I was in awe of the experience. I could go back home now because the terror was released. One of the questions I asked was, "God, what was the purpose of all the fear?" I was told, "I knew that you would release all your fear to me," I understood that answer. I had been guided to a state of mind where I could release all my fear. I had to choose between my fears and my life. I chose life.

After the fifteen hours were over, I could only hold

the special state of mind necessary to communicate with this higher life force for small periods of time. With each instance of communication, the time I was able to hold this contact increased until I was able to hold it for weeks at a time.

Each time the energy would come I would feel a physical shift in my consciousness. Total love and total peace encompassed my being. Each time the shift in my consciousness occurred I felt no worry, no fear. The frequency at which I lived and the frequency at which the God force energy resided seemed to come closer. The shock to my physical being became less and less until, many years later, I have become one with the energy.

I think this is what the voice meant when I was told, "Unite your body and your soul. I'll show you the way."

"Lord take me from this, this is more than I can stand."

By Winston

On July 15, 1992, I spoke these words in my mind and was instantly transported from the pain of being on fire from the waist up.

My wife, Roberta, had just returned from a hiking trip with some friends. She had taken our houseguest, Felicia, and her six-year-old daughter, Rebecca, up to the Walk of the Flowers trail on Mt. Adams, the 12,252-ft. hopefully-extinct volcano, which is the dominating presence of the Trout Lake Valley in southwest Washington. As Roberta came back into town with Felicia she saw two people in their mid-thirties with a gasoline can trying to hitchhike back up the mountain. Hitching a ride late on a mid-week afternoon twelve miles up the remote, rough, mostly one-lane road to where their old car had run out of gas was going to be an almost impossible task. Roberta told them she would be back and run them up to where they had left their car as soon as she delivered our guests back home.

When she came and told me about the couple, I volunteered to take them up the hill. After I picked up the hitchhikers, and we started the hour-and-a-half drive back up the mountain, I learned little about them except that they weren't married. The woman was visiting from Texas, and the man was more-or-less self-employed as a television camera operator in Hood River. The trip was without incident, and we eventually reached their fifteen-year-old Mercedes sedan that had obviously seen better days.

The man poured the gasoline into the car, and tried to start it up. The starter worked fine but the engine wouldn't engage. I suggested we pour a little gasoline into the air intake. We got some gasoline from the tank by unhooking the gas tank line, raised the hood and removed the air cleaner. I had about a cup of gasoline in a small can, which I dribbled slowly into the air intake while the man tried unsuccessfully several times to start the car.

It was very warm; in the nineties, no wind was blowing. We were getting low on gasoline, there was enough for one more attempt. This time, as I started to pour in the gas, the car backfired through the intake, igniting all of the fumes that had collected under the hood. The explosion blew the gasoline in the small cup I was holding all over my shirt. Instantly I was on fire from the waist up. The pain was indescribably intense. The sound of the flames thundered in my ears and I was screaming. I remember reaching a point of total desperation and thinking the words, "Lord take me from this, this is more than I can stand."

Immediately, I was transported to a place of painlessness. I was above the earth in space. I could look out and see the universe much as it looks on a clear, moon-

less night. My body was still screaming, and I was aware
that it was still on fire. I had been removed from all pain
per my request. A wide beam of red laser-like light
stretched from my body on earth to the farthest reaches
of the universe. I seemed to have instantly become a
much larger entity connected to information, perceptions, and awareness far beyond anything I had experienced. I received, in a matter of seconds, a hyper-burst
of essential information concerning what I needed to do
when I was returned to my body. This information was
not in the form of speech. Speech would have been too
slow. Any question or directed thought concerning what
was to happen next was simply supplied with the
knowingness of how, when, what, and where.
I knew that:

* I would be returned to my body momentarily.
* I would be totally in charge until I got to the hospital.
* I would be given enough strength to get to the
  emergency room in Hood River, Oregon.
* Hood River Hospital would send me to a regional
  burn center in Portland, Oregon.
* I would be out of the hospital in two weeks.
* There would be no major long-term problems with
  my healing.
* There would be some scars, but no one would
  notice them unless I called them to their attention.
* My friend, Jerry Stone, would be the one to drive
  me the twenty-five miles to the emergency room in

Hood River, because he would not be afraid to drive fast, and he would be far more detached than my wife, Roberta.

* I was aware that the body and mind which I knew as Winston was but a small portion of this much larger, more powerful being that I was in space. In this pain-free place I occupied, I seemed to have unlimited access to past and future events simultaneously.

* I also knew that I wouldn't be able to take all the power and information back with me, because my earthly body and mind were not capable of containing the energy of the super-being I had become.

* I knew that in that place I was a child of the universe with the ability to travel any place instantly by thought.

I was not overly excited to return to my burnt body and endure the weeks and months of physical pain that were to follow, but it was required. My earth mission was not yet over. What I had yet to experience could only be experienced at the micro-level of a human body. In space I felt unattached from emotion. I had total understanding of everything that crossed my mind but I did not experience emotion as I normally felt it in my physical body. That was why I had to go back.

This experience transpired in the span of one continuous scream, because I never stopped to inhale until the fire was put out. As a result, I didn't burn my lungs.

I am a trained opera singer and brass player, and I could probably scream continuously for something between thirty seconds to a minute. I was hoarse for two weeks and had some problems with my voice for some time after the accident. The other two people who were there said that my scream was a sound they could never forget.

When I returned to my body, seconds later, I was lying on my back in the middle of the road. The man was throwing dirt on me. My eyes and mouth were full of dirt. I was spitting as I got up from the ground. I was in a great deal of pain but I could control it and deal with it. We had to get going down the mountain. The woman was shaken by the experience and didn't feel that she could drive me down the road. Her boyfriend needed to stay with the Mercedes. It was still stalled on a blind curve, and we were concerned about it causing an accident.

I told her she had to drive because I could not. My hands had been close to the flash (gasoline flashes at something like seven or eight hundred degrees) of the explosion and were incapable of grasping a steering wheel. I told her she would be able to do this and that I needed to get to the Hood River Hospital as quickly as possible. She fearfully took the wheel and we started down the hill, honking to pass cars in turnouts as we overtook them. I kept talking to her, encouraging her to keep going, and not to drive too fast. After several miles, she stretched her hand and touched my leg for a moment, more, somehow to reassure herself rather than to comfort me.

The woman related her story to my wife several days later. She told Roberta that as a result of this experience she had to re-evaluate all that she believed. At first she'd felt suspicious that I had helped them, because she couldn't understand why I would do something with no possible gain for myself. She felt guilty because she had not helped put out the flames, afraid that she would catch fire herself. She only reluctantly drove off the mountain. She later said she was prompted to touch my leg while driving—a bizarre impulse that her rational mind tried to ignore. When she touched my leg a stream of energy, strength, and courage flowed from my body through hers, giving her the ability to drive like she never believed possible. She claimed to have seen angels who helped her down the mountain.

When we arrived at our home, I told Roberta to call the Hood River Hospital and Jerry Stone. Jerry was four miles away. My right ear had sort of melted; burnt skin was hanging in sheets from my neck and face. My hands were black. The fluids from the seeping burns had combined with the gray volcanic dust that had been used to extinguish the fire and I appeared to be dripping mud. I looked charred from the waist up. Felicia's five-year-old daughter didn't recognize me; she thought I was a monster.

Roberta drove to Jerry Stone's and he got behind the

wheel. We made the forty-five minute trip to the hospital in something less than thirty minutes. I walked into the hospital emergency room, and they showed me to a table. The pain I had been controlling for an hour and a half all came pressing in. The emergency room nurse and doctor were trying to get readings for blood pressure, pulse, etc. I was shaking all over with pain. The electronics would not register. They gave me a Demerol shot and told me I could have another in five minutes. After two more shots, which seemed to have no effect, they gave me a shot of morphine. Within seconds all pain disappeared and I was able to answer their admittance questions, comment about my pain status, and raise the issue of their sending me to the regional burn center in Portland.

I was a borderline choice for the burn center because I didn't quite pass the severity index for admission to Emmanuel's Burn Center. The index is based on the percentage of body area and amount of second- and third-degree burns sustained. My third-degree burns were relatively small in area: several patches on my chest, abdomen, and the inside of my right arm. My hands had pretty serious second-degree burns, my right ear and the skin under my chin had been burned quite badly. What tipped the scale in my favor was the fact that the fire on my body had been extinguished with dirt, and that raised the possibility of infection dramatically. Also, I kept insisting that I wanted to be sent to the burn center in Portland per my out-of body instructions.

As soon as I was stabilized, I was sent by ambulance to the Emmanuel Burn Center. My trip to Portland was uneventful; I passed the time talking to the Emergency Medical Technicians. When we arrived at the hospital, I went on record by telling the nurses and doctors that I would be out of there in two weeks. The head nurse took Roberta aside and told her not to expect me to be able to get out quite so soon because my burns were quite severe.

The doctors operated almost immediately, and I awoke the next morning wrapped in bandages. I knew, from a previous experience with an injury, about the twice-daily dressing changes and the debriding of burn patients. Debriding is the scrubbing of burn sites with gauze pads to both remove old skin and stimulate new growth. It is a long-standing burn treatment and extremely painful. I'd observed someone else being debrided and I remembered thinking that the pain caused by the treatment seemed to be much worse than the pain of the burn itself.

So when the nurse gave me my dressing-change painkillers that first morning, I asked about debriding. I was greatly relieved to find out that Dr. Parshley, the head of the Burn Center, had changed the burn treatment policy. He and his staff did not debride burns daily because the patient trauma was so great. They had found that it did not seem to improve the patient's recovery time. Debriding, if it became necessary, was done under a general anesthetic. I was greatly relieved to be in one of the few places where this new policy was in effect, and offered up a small prayer of thanks that this was where I had been advised to come.

When the dressings came off I assessed the damage in a mirror. I was impressed that I looked so much better than I had when I'd arrived the night before, and it did seem possible that I might get to go home in a couple of weeks. My only job while there was to get well and heal as quickly as possible. School started in less than six weeks and I wanted to be there on the first day. We had just moved to Trout Lake in April, where I had been a long-term substitute. I liked my teaching situation and had been pleased to be offered a regular contract for the coming year.

Roberta told me that morning that she had called family and friends, and within twenty-four to forty-eight hours I was on multiple prayer lists in various parts of the country. I was aware even that first morning that the room seemed to be charged with healing energy. The man sharing the room with me had been severely burned on his legs when a spray paint can hidden in a pile of leaves he was burning exploded, coating his legs with burning, sticky paint. He was unresponsive and being fed through a tube. Although he had been there for three or four months, he became much better in several days and was moved to rehabilitation by the end of the week, and was released to go home the following week. The nurses and staff were surprised and pleased with his rapid transition from irrationality and inability to feed himself to relative normalcy within a matter of days.

I had a slight setback toward the end of the first week, infection set in, and my temperature shot up for several days. I was placed on a powerful I.V. antibiotic. My memories of those days are quite hazy; part of the time I was delirious.

The second man to share my room had been splashed by slag in an aluminum plant. His burns were small in area but very deep. After a week one of the nurses remarked to my wife that whoever was in the room with Winston seemed to heal quicker than normal. I was also healing quickly. I spent a lot of time visualizing white light and healing energy filling the room and overflowing from there to the rest of the hospital, city, state, nation, world, and universe.

At the end of exactly two weeks, I was sent home. Roberta learned how to change the dressing, and I was released. My burns were not yet healed and the inside of my right hand and several patches on my chest would require skin grafts. I was happy with my rapid progress, but having multiple skin grafts or twice daily dressing changes for the next six to eight weeks was not something I wanted to think about. Having endured a skin graft before, I did not relish the idea of doing it again. Imagine the worst sunburn you have ever had or could conceive of — not only where the burn occurred but also at the graft donor site - continuously, twenty-four hours a day, for weeks.

The next day, Friday, after praying for guidance and courage, I went back for skin grafts on Saturday and was released on Sunday. I was able to report for teaching that fall, even though I wore elastic gauntlets for several months to reduce scarring on my hands.

Several months later I was completely healed, and what scarring I now have is totally unnoticeable unless I call attention to it. I am changed by the experience and am still integrating the whole event. I definitely do not want to be burned again. The experience of being in my soul or spirit body and possessing almost infinite knowingness changed my life in a number of ways. I have analyzed it many times. Why did it happen? What did I learn as a result? How does it connect with the other spiritual experiences of my life?

One day, several months after being burned, I was walking through the Target store in Portland's Clackamas Mall. I had no specific reason to be shopping there, but I felt pulled to go there on my way to my car in the parking lot. I moved through the aisles quickly, and was passing the book section when my eye was drawn to a book on an upper shelf. It was not a particularly note-worthy cover, but I was drawn to that specific book with almost alarming strength. It was Betty Eadie's, *Embraced by the Light*. I knew beyond reason that I was supposed to buy this book; it had information paralleling my own experience.

I took the book home and was thrilled to find the account of angels answering laser-light-like prayer emissions from earth. I realized that the experience I'd had after uttering my supplication, "Lord, take me from this; this is more than I can stand," was a confirmation and explanation that I had immediate access whenever I needed it. What an empowering idea! I have read her book many times. I have multiple copies that I lend to anyone who seems interested. I share my own story with those people who seem to be seeking something. Since the burning, I often receive strong intuitive nudges about books to read, reasons for why my students may be misbehaving, predictions of future outcomes. It comes as "knowingness." I often seem to be at the right place at the right time. I know that I have personal guidance that helps me steer my course.

The burning incident on top of Mt. Adams ended a fifteen-year spiritual search. I had been reading books on Eastern philosophies, New Age, channeling, out-of-body experiences, Edgar Cayce, to mention a few. The traditional Christian faith with which I was raised did not seem to offer me specific, personal answers to questions I had about why I was here, what was my purpose, what was I supposed to do, etcetera.

I thought back to a previous spiritual encounter, twenty-five years earlier. Roberta and I were planning to be married in several months. It was a Friday afternoon. I was home from teaching school and had called Roberta's sorority house to make arrangements for what we were going to do for the weekend. I had heard from one of my roommates that she had been seen riding around in a sport car with some guy from the college choir. This filled me with uncontrollable feelings of jealously. I was distraught with the idea that she was out with someone else. I called every place I could think of in an attempt to reach her. It seems a small thing to be upset about now, but at the time I was livid. My room-mates had left for the weekend and I had the apartment to myself. I wanted answers, and I had tried all that I could think of to do except prayer. That was the only thing I had not tried.

I went into the small bedroom with two sets of bunk beds that the four of us shared and lay down on my back. To no one in particular, I said that if there really was a God in heaven, if Jesus was the final answer for all things, then I wanted some sign that someone was listening to me. I wanted answers about this situation. Since my roommates would be away, I was resolved to spend the entire weekend in that dark bedroom waiting for an answer. I also went so far as to say that if I received no answers then I would wash my hands of all I had been taught in church and Sunday school. I fully expected to spend most of the weekend fruitlessly waiting for an answer or sign; it came within minutes.

The dark bedroom filled with light. A bearded being in a white robe came to me. I could not look at him without shading my eyes. I was assured nonverbally that my worry and concern was all for nothing. I was given peace. I was no longer concerned. I had the impression of being lovingly reprimanded for my lack of faith. This being knew me intimately, and I had the impression that I like Peter in the Bible, would reveal flaws in my faith in the future but that this being would remain constant, regardless. It was a wonderful, humbling experience.

Later that evening I talked to Roberta and we went out together. I was subdued and felt sheepish to think of my jealous reaction. One would think that this kind of experience would shape one's spiritual outlook for the rest of his life, but it did not. I could not forget the experience, but I could choose to not think about it very often.

Several months before being burned in 1992, I remember looking up to a clear night sky and sending a prayer asking that my spiritual growth be accelerated, even if it meant hardship. I had been exploring all aspects of spiritual thought for years and had not found answers that gave me peace. Reflection and contemplation since I was burned have brought me to the realization that the earlier spiritual episode in my life was directly connected to the event on Mt. Adams. I could not have had the faith to ask that I be delivered from the pain of burning gasoline had I not had the school-days experience of an almost immediate response to a fervent prayer. I know that in both situations I was heard and I know that I am loved beyond reason or understanding. That is what grace is about. I wasn't trying to be particularly good. I didn't do anything to deserve it. Grace is. It is available all the time. Asking honestly from the bottom of one's heart is all that has to be done.

I receive guidance daily on all sorts of things. I can exercise my free will, because that is God's gift of making me in his image. I am allowed to experiment, much as a good parent allows his children to make inappropriate choices, knowing that they will learn from them. If I ask, I receive. It is immediate if needed. Judgment seems to be more a creation of man than of God. He functions beyond the confines of time and space. Everyone is granted grace beyond reason or understanding. We are all saved. The flesh-and-blood body I exist in here on earth is but a small, temporary part of a larger awareness that is connected directly to all of God's creation.

My burning in 1992 at age fifty is the genesis of all of my other stories. Since that episode I have been driven to examine and record the other times I have experienced outside intervention. That event is the filter by which I gauge the other experiences; It was a beginning of my developing awareness. Not all my touches with intervention are included here because I judge some of them less noteworthy. Most of my earlier or subsequent experiences were less threatening and dramatic.

Someone less hardheaded or obtuse than I am would probably not have needed so many wake-up calls. I was like the mule in the story of the farmer who sold a good, hard-working mule to one of his neighbors. The neighbor tried everything but couldn't make the mule work, so he took the mule back to the seller, complaining loudly. Whereupon the original owner picked up a stout stick and slammed it down hard, right between the eyes of his old mule and lightly remarked, "He's a real good mule, you just got to get his attention first."

I had previously had multiple close calls — being hit by a tree and a Buick. God finally got my attention. I am resolved to be a "good" mule. Now, I don't need or have to be amazed. Through this experience I have progressed from "I believe" to "I know." Both my request to be advanced spiritually and my quest for answers were granted.

The Voice Within

Within a year of being burned, I seemed to be tasked with recording the memories of that experience while they were still fresh in my mind. That led to my thinking and writing the following stories that are the two earliest times I could remember being given caring advice.

Winston

Hypothermia, a Peaceful Way to Die
By Winston

My first real memory of having a voice seemingly apart from me speak in my mind dates back to when I was sixteen or seventeen. I was an avid hunter, having started at age twelve with my grandfather. Elmer Lot Howard (Grandpa Howard) was a brave man to introduce young Winston to hunting with shotgun and deer rifle, but he had already performed this rite of passage for his sons and a five-years-older cousin. I thought of it as my major occupation outside of school during the fall. I hunted for grouse and ducks before and after school during September and October, and for deer during November. Where we lived in the country there were grouse, deer and bear. In order to find ducks it was necessary to drive for ten or fifteen minutes. I filled the freezer with game birds each season. I looked forward to each weekend of hunting with Grandpa, schoolmates, or just by myself.

One particularly wet, miserable day of gloppy snow interspersed with rain — typical north Idaho winter weather — I was hunting by myself on the Wyman ranch, just south of Naples, Idaho. I was several miles from the house, cold, wet, and tired. The temperature was somewhere around 32 degrees. My grandfather had not talked to me about hypothermia. I didn't know what it was until years later, sometime after I was an adult.

The pins-and-needles feelings in my hands and feet had faded, and I was filled with a euphoric feeling of warmth and drowsiness. It was still early in the day and I was still planning to spend the whole day hunting, but I was cold and wet. The mile-and-a-half to two-mile walk back to the house would require a hard walk through foot-deep snow. I sat down against a stump under a tree out of the rain. I felt wonderful, but I wanted to take just a little nap before I trudged back to the house. I had been lucky to find this pleasant stump under a sheltering tree. I closed my eyes. I felt relaxed and comfortable. My head dropped forward and I dozed for a short time. I awoke suddenly to the seemingly spoken thought: "If you go to sleep again, then this stump will be where they will find your body." I forced myself to get up and start moving; it was a major effort of will to leave my nap. Within minutes, my hands and feet hurt worse than before, but I continued to force myself to walk the several miles back to warmth, safety, food, and hot chocolate.

I didn't know until years later that I had experienced the classic symptoms of hypothermia. When I was out there alone, I couldn't think of anything I wanted to do more than just sit on that stump and go to sleep. I can't explain why I woke up. Was it some inner sense of self-preservation? Was it the voice of a guardian angel or higher power? It was my first memory of hearing a voice in my mind that seemed apart from my regular thoughts. I didn't think much about it at the time. I know now that I came very close to dying that day but for the words spoken in my head. It would have been a calm and peaceful way to die.

I have since thought of this incident in reference to euthanasia. If I were sick with incurable disease or unable to experience the wonder of life, would this be a possible and peaceful solution for unending pain and suffering? There are times that voices apart from me seem to speak in my head. I consider myself normal. Doesn't everyone hear voices that seem to come from outside themselves?

The Burgundy Jaguar
By Winston

I hear voices from time to time. This is the second
time I remember it happening because I was answered so
quickly. It was not a life-threatening or even an important event, but I remember it clearly almost forty years
later.

I was about twenty-three years old, walking downtown in Moscow, Idaho. As a young man, money being
no object, the car of choice for me would have been a
Jaguar 4-door sedan. I had earlier wandered into a
showroom in Spokane where the smooth lines, leather
seats, tasteful wood dash, elegant gauges all appealed to
me. As I was walking down the street in Moscow, Idaho,
a burgundy-colored Jaguar with leather upholstery
ghosted past me as I stood standing on the curb. I posed
a question as a thought in my head with a lot of energy,
"Will I ever in my lifetime have the resources to possess
such a car?" The answer from someone or someplace
other than me was immediate and specific: "Yes, but not
until middle age and by that time it will not be your car
of choice."

At the time I was struck by the immediate response
to what I knew was a somewhat frivolous question. I did
want to know if my planned profession of being a musi-
cian/ teacher would provide with me a comfortable
living. I thought about the immediacy and obvious

wisdom of the answer. Since it was the second major time I had heard a voice, I started to rely on this personal guidance. It has become an important part of my life. I know that if I want information and if I ask with the energy of my heart, I will get an answer as a voice or vision or some personal message that will enable me to make a good choice. In my teaching this guidance sometimes comes unbidden: a student may misbehave and I need to respond immediately with some discipline. In this situation, I am ready and about to write a referral and send the student to the office when a voice says to me, "You don't know what happened this morning before this student left home." I immediately change my discipline plans, take the student aside, and ask him or her: "What's going on? This does not seem like you. Do you need to talk to someone?" or something to kindly diffuse the situation.

I have an established rapport with my guidance system; I don't think I could teach without it. I think most teachers develop some inner sense or feeling that guides them. The incident with the burgundy Jaguar helped establish that rapport for me. As a mature adult, I could probably scrape the resources together to buy a Jaguar, but it certainly would not be my car of choice. I want a car that I can get repaired almost anyplace, not an exotic machine. I have a fondness for Jaguars because of the memory they stimulate of a connection to guidance. I can have help for anything, large or small, frivolous or important. All I have to do is to remember to ask from my heart.

Remembering to ask is the hard part. One has to give up ego and humbly admit that help is needed.

Requests for Divine Help

My stories in this section are about times when I was consciously using the divine request formula. The successful outcome of all of these encounters paved the way for my faith to grow. It also was the first time my husband ventured into my spiritual realm.   Dolora

Prayers are answered, but not always in ways or the time that we expect. The incident I describe in this section happened in a matter of hours, and was surprising to me in terms of its foresight and depth.   Winston

Courage to Fly
By Dolora

My children, Wendy and Ryan, were seven and three respectively. Steve, my husband, was working for Pan American World Services, a division of Pan American World Airways, and the year was 1978. I had decided to take the children and try flying stand-by to Boise to see my husband's parents. This was new to me. I had never had the courage to do the stand-by thing by myself with two children without Steve's help. It was a short flight with no stopovers, so being bumped was not a possibility once I got on the plane. This trip to Boise was going to be quite an adventure for me. Steve was in Boston on a training session and I was on my own.

I had arranged with my friend Kathy to drive us to the Winslow ferry. I had also arranged with another friend in Seattle, Marilyn, to pick up our entourage from the ferry and deposit us at Sea-Tac International Airport. All went well and we arrived at the gate for our Alaska Airlines flight headed for Boise. I kept asking my angels to please help us get on the flight. "Please let us board the plane," I prayed. I did not have a back-up plan for getting home. Flying was new to me, let alone flying stand-by with two young children who could be seated in any available seat in the plane, not necessarily next to me. Wendy, the seven-year-old, had been briefed and could handle herself well. She was a very focused child and would read or entertain herself quietly. Ryan was only three and really needed to be with me. We had made a study of the best times to travel as a "non-rev(enue)" and this was a low-impact time, the best day to start our adventure. We had no problem getting on the flight. We arrived in Boise right on schedule. My angels had done a very good job.

Grandma and Grandpa met us at the airport and my confidence level in being able to travel by myself was certainly boosted.

I had never been really on my own. I'd gone from living with my parents in a small town in Idaho to living in a sorority in college. The sorority rules at that time were very strict. We had to be in the house every school night by ten-thirty although on weekends we could stay out until one AM. It did not pay be late or you would get locked out. From the sorority I went into marriage, with never a time to learn to depend on myself, to be responsible for myself.

Wendy and Ryan loved visiting their grandparents in Boise. The place abounded with toys, ancient magical toys that Grandma had saved from her children's youth. Grandma always had fresh cookies with perfect frosting and you could sit on the kitchen counters and help her roll out the dough. You could even sneak bites of cookie dough and never get scolded. Grandma Deal's kitchen was pink and always filled with wonderful smells. She would get down on the floor with you and giggle and laugh, playing silly paper dolls or letting you create a large farm with all the toy animals — barns and fencing included.

Going to Grandma Deal's house was truly an adventure in self-indulgence if you were a child or just one at heart. There was even a restaurant she would take you too for lunch that had telephones at every booth. You could call up the waitress and just order whatever your taste buds wanted that day. Fun was always the top priority, and as a parent it brought me joy to watch my children be so free and happy.

The journey to Boise had gone perfectly so far and the rest of the plan was that Ryan and I would fly home from Boise to Seattle and be there before Steve arrived home from Boston. I had not made arrangements for transportation to get from Sea-Tac Airport to Poulsbo, but I knew I could figure something out. I wasn't just being naïve; I just wasn't sure which flight we would get from Boise. Wendy was going to stay a while longer with her grandmother and then the two of them were going to have the adventure of riding the train from Boise to Seattle later in the week.

The sun was beaming and the weather was perfect. Grandpa Deal drove us to the airport. The flight was really full and there were only a few seats left for stand-by passengers. The gate attendant had filled all the seats but one. My name was called and I went to the podium praying, as this was the only scheduled Alaska Airlines flight going to Seattle that day. Ryan was standing mutely by my side. The gate attendant informed me that there was only one seat left on the flight and it was in first class, and if I wanted to take the flight I would have to purchase a twenty-dollar upgrade. However, there was no room for Ryan. I had to make this flight in order to be home before Steve. I was also aware that children over the age of two were not allowed to fly without a seat assignment. I was in a quandary as to my next step. The gatekeeper asked me how old my son was. I stated that he was three years old.

The gatekeeper again asked me how old my son was and I replied with a question in my voice. "How old would you like him to be?" The gate attendant allowed my "two-year-old son" and me to board the plane and take the last remaining seat. I was seated next to a gentleman named Butch Maki. His mother had given me piano lesson in Bonners Ferry when I was a young girl. He helped me with all the fishing gear Steve had requested I bring home.

When it came time for breakfast to be served, the flight attendant remarked that Ryan and I would not be getting anything because we were stand-by passengers. Butch kindly gave my hungry three-year-old his breakfast. We arrived at Sea-Tac safe and sound. Ryan and I dashed for the shuttle to the ferry terminal with Butch bringing up the rear carrying all the fishing gear that I couldn't handle. We made the ferry with ten minutes to spare.

Winslow appeared on the horizon and we disembarked the ferry, struggling with all the gear, and hiked up the long ramp to the terminal. I had no idea how we were going to get the ten miles from Winslow to Poulsbo, but I could always call a taxi. Much to our surprise a shuttle bus had just started running that week from the Bainbridge Island ferry terminal to Poulsbo and, believe it or not, the bus was waiting for us as we walked down the ramp.

I was in awe. Ryan, all the luggage and I had made it home from Boise in four hours with the help of a compassionate gate attendant, an old acquaintance, a new bus schedule, and faith. This may not seem like much in the overall big picture of things, but it was huge magic for me.

I had accomplished this on my own and I gained tremendous confidence that my life was always in "Divine Order." I will always be grateful for the perfect timing the angels provided for this expansion of my ability to adventure.

207 Sunrise
By Dolora

The summer of 1989 brought many changes and a
test of our faith. We had moved to Sun Valley, Idaho, in
the fall of 1988 and rented a house in the Elkhorn area,
but we had to be out by the first of August because the
people who owned it were coming back from New York.
We had spent six months looking for a house we could
afford to buy. I was willing to accept anything that had
at least two baths, three bedrooms, a garage, a place for
me to sew and, of course, the usual additional parts of a
house including a kitchen, living room a place to do
laundry, etc.

Prices were much higher than in the Seattle area and
we were having difficulty finding anything we could
afford. The housing market was so tight that there were
bidding wars over houses. A reasonably priced house
might be on the market for three days. My frustration
was complete and I got really mad at my angels. I had
done my part by continually searching and I just wasn't
getting any help. I had looked at every house in the
Valley under one hundred and fifty thousand dollars,
which was the maximum we could afford.

I sat down in meditation and really screamed mentally at the angelic help I didn't feel I was receiving. We
— the angels and I — started having a two-way dialogue. They asked me why I needed a house. I ex-

plained that as a human being it was necessary to have a place to sleep, a place to take a bath, and a place to put your stuff. As a human you need these things to survive. I explained that without food, shelter and clothing (the bare necessities of life) it was very difficult to be a spiritual being.

The next morning my husband woke up and said I should call everyone in our neighborhood and see if they would be willing to sell their house. I was getting desperate as August was rapidly approaching and I had no place to put my family. I called the Elkhorn Association and asked for the list of homeowners in the Sunrise area where we were renting. I immediately started calling absentee owners to see if they might be interested in selling their house. The second person I called lived in Twin Falls, Idaho, and he said, "Yes, I might be interested in selling the house." He was building a large house in Twin Falls and they didn't travel to Sun Valley very frequently. For some strange reason I asked the owner of the house, his name was Jerry, if he knew a young man from Twin Falls I had dated in high school.

Jerry asked me how I knew this man. I explained that I had met him at music camp during the summer of 1959. Well, my friend turned out to be Jerry's cousin. Jerry sold me the house. It wasn't on the market; no realtor fees were involved. The house was the exact same floor plan as the house we had been renting, except it was two houses down the street. All of my requirements had

been met. Three bedrooms, 2 baths, all the other necessary features, plus a loft for me to sew in, and the price
was under $150,000.

Steve was laid off from his job in July, but we made
the decision to stay here because Wendy had only one
year of high school left. We had moved her the year
before and we did not have the heart to move her again.
We looked at our savings account and decided that we
could manage for at least a year.

We bought the little house in Sunrise even with Steve
not having a regular income. The bank allowed us
ninety five percent financing which was miraculous. It
was only three days from the time I told my angels why I
needed a house until I had one under contract to buy. I
expressed my gratitude to the angels. When they understood my need, and I put a lot of genuine emotion into
my request, I had a house the next day. The lesson here
for me was that we can have anything we desire if we get
truly clear about what we want. Our emotion becomes
the fuel that propels our creations into existence almost
instantaneously if the emotions are strong enough you
release all doubt. I cherish my little house in Sunrise
because it feels like home. I believe my house was a gift
from the angels, and it has been ever since. Thank You.

Direct Petition
By Winston

All of my stories, with the exception of, "Lord take me from this, this is more than I can stand," indicate an unasked protective response or reaction to something that happened to me. This one is different because I clearly asked for help and it came within hours, precisely when it was needed.

During 1981 fall semester, I withdrew from the University of Texas because the scholarship I had expected did not materialize. We had moved to Texas from Polson, Montana, after two years teaching because my contract had not been renewed. I never knew exactly why, but I wasn't surprised; there had been friction between the administration and me over a number of issues. I was Polson's fourth band teacher in seven years; no one had stayed very long. I had not yet come up for tenure and they were under no obligation to give me reasons. I was called into the superintendent's office late in February and simply given the option of resigning. Some representatives from parents came forward and offered to help me fight the administration's decision, but I felt teaching would never be the same for me in Polson. I was asked to interview for a music teaching position in nearby Thompson Falls but decided to go back to school and work on my doctorate in Opera Theater. I sent tapes and letters of inquiry to the University of Indiana at Bloomington and the University of Texas at Austin and received positive responses in regard to scholarship possibilities from both. Since I would be a non-resident, any assistance would help. I chose the University of Texas because tuition was cheaper and it seemed to be closer to a number of professional opportunities to perform in Houston, Dallas, Fort Worth, and San Antonio.

We arrived in Texas after the fall semester had started; I would not become an official student until winter. I sang with the opera workshop that fall and started studying with Jess Walters; it was my first opportunity to study with a fellow baritone. I became an official non-resident student immediately after Christmas. It was my understanding that a scholarship would be forthcoming the following fall provided they liked me as a student. I figured it was an almost sure thing: I had professional credentials, I had already done most of the course work at the University of Washington, and I was a mature singer.

It was a busy semester. I was taking a full load, understudying the role of Rodrigo in Verdi's "Don Carlo," performing the title role of Puccini's Gianni Schicchi and singing Poulenc's "Le Bal Masque" with the New Music Ensemble. There were graduate students with scholarships who weren't doing as much. I also had an affair with a young, beautiful, twenty-two-year-old voice student whom I met at a party. She opened the conversation by telling me I was not like the other men in the music department and ended up by kissing me. I was vulnerable and stupid. It ended after several months with a confrontation between my wife, the young woman, and myself. Roberta told her that she loved me too and she had prior claim. The affair was ended shortly thereafter by the young woman. I was humbled; I didn't want this to happen again. I didn't think my marriage would survive another similar episode.

Late in the semester the head of the Opera Department stepped down and was replaced by someone who had not made any promises to me concerning potential scholarships. Music schools and graduate schools in general being gossip factories, the new department head had probably heard that I'd been involved with an undergraduate. He was under no obligation to honor his predecessor's promises. The head of the choral department liked my singing and offered me a scholarship to sing in his groups and enter the choral program. It was not the direction I wanted to go. I decided to seek professional singing situations and say to hell with academia. I also wanted to get away and think. I needed to wrestle with things that had happened.

A very short time after I decided to leave the University of Texas, I happened to see a notice posted elsewhere than the music department for auditions to be held for a touring production of Frank Loesser's "Most Happy Fella," to be held at the University in several weeks. My voice had previously been compared to the original Broadway star Robert Weede. I found a copy of the score in the library and realized that this role fit both my voice and temperament. I took it to my coach and teacher and learned the role in several weeks in anticipation of the upcoming auditions. I had communicated with the producers of the tour that I wanted to try out for the lead. A week or so before the audition I learned that the part of Tony would be sung by Rod McWerther from the Metropolitan Opera. I called the producers and told them that I was still interested in doing some smaller parts and being a cover in case something happened to Mr. McWerther. The role was so big; it took fifty-five minutes just to sing all the music without the dialogue. I didn't think anyone would want to sing a matinee and an evening performance in the same day so I made singing the matinees part of the proposed deal. I would sing several small parts, the postman, the priest, the doctor, and the lead role of Tony in the matinees. Chorus members would cover the small parts when I sang the lead. I auditioned and they accepted my terms. I would be off to Florida immediately after Christmas to rehearse the show. This would get me back into professional singing. I could possibly arrange for a director or an agent to hear me and I would start getting some more contracts.

Rod McWerther had not arrived for the first days of rehearsal so I was allowed to rehearse in his place. As soon as he appeared I was not allowed any more rehearsal as the lead. I quickly got to know the other cast members. I was particularly attracted to Celia, who played the part of Marie, Tony's bossy, unsympathetic, sister. She was saucy and outrageously outspoken. Of the sixteen men in the cast I was the only married man; Rod McWerther was divorced. I enjoyed being around Celia, she was fun, and I was physically attracted to her. I was concerned, though, to not repeat the affair of the previous spring. One evening, I met her unexpectedly outside the motel where most of the cast was staying. I had a sort of vision that she and I were standing on opposite sides of a deep dark chasm. Visions have come to me several times in my life (see "A Golden Vision" and "Finding a New Wife"). In my visions time seems to stop, I am wide awake but experiencing a vivid dream. I am able to remember clearly; meaning and interpretation come later. These dreams or visions have all had important personal messages that seem to come from someplace other than my normal consciousness.

This particular awake dream was not difficult for me to interpret considering my previous history. I was attracted to this woman, but trying to cross the chasm between us was likely to involve unpleasant long-term consequences for us both. My marriage would probably not survive. Celia and I spent a lot of time together in the course of the following rehearsal period and tour. We sat together on the bus, and ate together in many restaurants. Most of the cast assumed we were sleeping together, but although we enjoyed our new friendship, physical intimacy did not occur.

Very early in the tour I sang a scheduled matinee. When it was announced that Winston Cook would be singing the part of Tony, the audience booed. I had had very little stage rehearsal in the part but the dialogue and music I knew well, but I was determined to do the best I could. At the end of the performance, I received a standing ovation from the audience when I took my solo bow. Rod McWerther, the lead, had watched the performance and told me he would be singing some auditions during the tour and that he felt comfortable with my doing some of his evening performances in addition to my contractual matinees.

My responsibilities to the tour grew even more when I accepted the position of acting road manager because the road manager fell in the orchestra pit, hurt his back, and had to leave the tour. I became the wake-up bad guy, luggage packer, schedule maintainer, and bus navigator, for which I received an extra stipend. I ended up doing five performances as the lead and twenty-some performances of the three small parts. One of our matinees was in Raleigh, North Carolina; I called ahead and invited the director of the National Opera Company (a small touring company) to come to my performance as Tony. He came backstage after my performance and told me to call him when the tour ended. The tour, with rehearsal, lasted approximately six weeks. Celia and I had become good friends and I kissed her goodbye and told her I would keep in touch by phone or letter. I returned to Austin, Texas. Celia went back to Boston.

I returned home on a Thursday, and called The National Opera Company on Friday. They informed me that they had to let one of their baritones go and asked if I could be in Raleigh the following week and sing the part of Frank, the prison warden in Strauss's "Die Fledermaus" the following Friday. It was a relatively small part but integral to the show. I accepted and made immediate practice arrangements with my piano coach, booked reservations for a flight leaving on Monday, bought a score, and started immediately to memorize the music and dialogue. On Saturday, auditions were being held for the annual Austin Parks and Recreation department's summer musical, which happened to be "Most Happy Fella."

I went to the audition Saturday morning and listened to a few people sing for the part of "Tony." My turn came and I sang "Mama, Mama," Tony's big aria and the dramatic solo recitative from the last act. After I sang, the auditions for the part of Tony were closed; I had the lead for the summer musical. The following week I went to Raleigh to sing the rest of their season, which would end in mid-May. I sang the performances of "Most Happy Fella" that summer and received the Austin Circle of Theater award for best actor in a musical. The Na-

tional Opera Company offered me a contract for the
following year.

While in Raleigh, I had a lot of time to write letters
to both my wife and Celia. I also made phone calls.
Our relationship grew as we found out more about each
other. My wife was not entirely comfortable with the
phone and letter communications that continued
through the summer while I was home.

The following fall I returned to Raleigh to spend
another season with the National Opera Company.
Roberta, my wife, became involved in a graduate music
education program so did not respond by mail with the
same frequency as Celia. I had a lot of time to write
letters, and make phone calls. Once you have learned
the music for a part, living and traveling from one performance to the next leaves a lot of time to fill. People's
Express, a now-defunct budget airlines was offering a
very low-cost round-trip airfare to eastern seaboard cities.
I asked my wife how she would feel about me taking a
cheap, short flight to Boston to see my friend Celia if I
got a couple of days off. She reluctantly agreed and I
went. I stayed in Celia's one-bedroom apartment. We
went to the No Name restaurant, the museum, and
walked around the historic sites to be seen. I rationalized
that going home to Austin, Texas, would cost more than
twice as much, and took at the very least half a day of
airtime each way. Celia and I had a great time. We did
not sleep together but I had some fantasies.

As the spring wore on, living and performing with the eleven other members of the company (two sopranos, two mezzos, two tenors, two baritones, and two basses, one technical and one musical director) became more and more tedious. Having a weekend meant to share a kitchen, bathrooms, the confines of the old house we lived in when were "home" in Raleigh. Celia and I continued to communicate. We shared almost everything about relationships, past and present. Celia had boyfriends, and I had a wife in Texas.

I took a second trip to Boston during the season. In the meantime my fantasies about what would happen during the weekend alone together had grown. I knew from some hints that the issue of sleeping together would be discussed and that I might have to make a decision that would dramatically affect my marriage or my relationship with Celia. As the airplane circled Logan International waiting to land, I wrestled with what I would say if Celia suggested we sleep together. I couldn't come up with any solution that would solve all the problems that could occur. I didn't want to turn down the opportunity to satisfy my fantasies, I didn't think my relationship with Celia would stay the same, I didn't know if my marriage would survive. I was stumped.

Finally, in desperation I asked God to just take over if this subject was discussed. I didn't think I was strong enough to refuse nor did I want to cause problems for Celia, my wife, or myself. Celia met me at the airport.

It was good to see her and hug her close. People's Express didn't serve meals; I was hungry. We went to dinner at a nearby inexpensive restaurant before going to her one-bedroom apartment. Being in close proximity charged the atmosphere with anticipation. Waiting for our food, Celia stated simply that she was thinking about sleeping with me that evening. Right or wrong I had fantasized about that moment many times. But without even thinking I heard myself give an immediate response, "I really would like to do that, but then our relationship changes and I become like most of the other men in your life. When I leave, everything will be different." It was a truly perfect answer. It communicated my feelings and concerns for our situation. It was totally unplanned and unexpected. I didn't feel in control of saying it. Celia changed the subject.

We ate our meal and planned what we would do for the rest of the weekend. Without any more discussion, Celia obviously made the decision that our continued friendship was more important to her than sleeping together. When we got to her apartment that evening, she got sheets and blankets and made up the couch. She slept in her bed and I slept on the couch, in wonder at how deftly everything had been resolved. I did have some mixed emotions as I lay on the couch. I still wanted Celia in a physical way but the evening's intervention directly after my direct petition for God's help was a clear message. Our relationship changed from that moment.

Three years later, Celia was at her wit's end with clinical depression. When I talked to her she seemed desperate. I was concerned that she might try suicide. I went to Boston again. I was able to help her through a bad weekend. Later, she was able to go into counseling and get professional help and medication. She had moved to a smaller studio apartment, which only had a bed and no couch. We shared the bed but all we did was sleep.

My relationship as friend and confidante to Celia continues twenty years later. It has grown to include her husband, Chris, and their three children, Alexander, Elenor, and Leah. This past July my heart warmed to see her two-year-old daughter, Leah, eat cookies while sitting next to Spencer our almost-two-year-old son.

Looking back I see that not only had I been supplied with multiple opportunities to sing, thus rebuilding my self-worth and confidence as a musician. I had also been provided with the challenge presented by a relationship with Celia. It forced me to think and grow. God, the great alchemist, had changed lead to gold. I was reminded to ask for God's help more often. I am glad I petitioned for his help.

The Phantom Road Grader

By Dolora

On January 23rd, 1996, we received a call from my husband's family telling us that his mother, who had been in an Alzheimer's unit in Boise for the previous two years, had just passed away. Emotionally we were happy that she no longer suffered in this physical form.

I had loved this woman very much. We had shared the joys of being moms, and a love of cooking, sewing and gardening. Every child in the universe who met Nell, my husband's mother, loved her. I was often intrigued by her ability to attract any child in any restaurant to her side. Nell gave living proof to the idea that anything or anyone we truly and openly love will always find our space.

We went through the process of the funeral and all that takes place at a time of grieving and releasing. All of this happened just after my car accident and Wendy's transfer to the University of Montana. We knew Wendy needed to get to Missoula to start school so that she could finish setting up her house on Lester Street. The weather had turned snowy and we were not comfortable with Wendy driving the mountain passes through Salmon, Idaho to Montana. Consequently, we put her on a plane to Missoula shortly after Nell's funeral, with the promise that her Dad would grab the first opportunity to drive her Volkswagen convertible to Missoula as soon as the weather cleared.

We returned home from Boise at noon on Sunday. The sun had been playing hide-and-seek all day. We checked the local weather report and it looked as if that moment was the only opportunity Steve would have to drive to Missoula without having to struggle through a blinding snowstorm. During good weather it takes about five-and-half hours to make the trip. Steve squeezed himself into the small space Wendy had left for driving her car and headed up Galena pass to Stanley. The weather started clouding up, but Steve decided to try my angel stuff and see if it worked. He asked the angels to keep his path clear, and each time he went around a curve in the road and the snow would start to fall, he requested help anew. Each time the sun came out and his path was clear.

Steve called me from Stanley, Idaho, with a weather update. He decided to continue the trip and headed on to Challis and Salmon. Frequently intervals of snow would start to fall and Steve would petition the angels to clear his way. Each time they did. Salmon appeared in the distance.

Dusk fell as Steve headed up Lost Trail Pass, the highest mountain pass on the trip. At this time the pass had not been improved and it was a very treacherous, winding road. The snow had started coming down with a vengeance. The highway had not yet been plowed and the little convertible was starting to spin and slip in the snowy conditions. The snow was now about a foot high and in the drifted areas was higher than the bumper. The car had to plow its way up the hill and often would lose traction while pushing the snow. Steve really needed some help and he needed it now. Prayer seemed the only answer.

Immediately a large road grader pulled out in front of Steve, and started moving up the hill, blade down, doing the job it was meant to do. The road grader, which did not appear to have any highway department markings, or the flashing "caution" lights found on most highway equipment, continued all the way to the top of the pass, pushing the snow out of Steve's way, producing a clear path in the snow. When they arrived at the summit the phantom road grader disappeared into the night. Steve could not even see where it had turned off the road. On subsequent trips up that pass we have looked and there is not a side road where the road grader could have disappeared.

Steve expressed his gratitude for the assistance in getting up the hill and drove safely down the other side of the pass just by the sheer force of gravity. Without ceremony he arrived in Darby and continued on into Missoula. I had told him how to find the little house on Lester Street. We had not been able to get in touch with Wendy as her phone was yet to be installed.

Exhausted, Steve arrived at the little yellow house to find it empty and all locked up. His frustration mounted as he realized he had no way to find Wendy or even unload the car. His cell phone had started functioning again somewhere around Darby, and he called to let me know of his dilemma.

I started asking my angels to have Wendy call home so I could tell her that her father was at her house. I rapidly sent her telepathic messages to "call home." In five minutes the phone rang; it was Wendy calling from a pay phone. She did not even know her father had left Sun Valley. Steve and Wendy soon connected, unloaded the car, and went out for a nice dinner. The next morning Wendy put her Dad on a plane for Sun Valley.

I have no doubt that we were being watched over and cared for at this time. and at every moment. Steve stretched his beliefs and asked for help from a force that was not physically tangible. He was indeed protected by some unseen benevolent power. The nice thing about this is that it allowed a space for Steve and I to connect on the same spiritual plane. His doubt about angelic help was cracked open a bit.

The lesson is clear, ask and you shall receive, particularly if you are open to receiving. Always, always be grateful, and express your gratitude for your blessings.

The Valley of the Shadow

Death is an interesting phenomenon that I have never been afraid of, just curious about. In each story in this section, I was conscious of a guiding force that was protecting me. Why? I believe we all have a coming in and going out suited to our growth. Dolora

I have had numerous close calls, many which could have resulted in my death. I have only recorded the most remarkable. Winston

Drowning
By Dolora

My Saint Bernard, Donner, just came and woke me
up. It was 2:50 in the morning. The valley had been
without rain for about two months and Donner and I
would pray for rain when we would take our walks. I
think Donner wanted me to know that the rain we had
been praying for was here. He asked to go outside just
for a brief moment. I accompanied him so I could feel
the moisture falling on my face. It was quite warm
outside, yet hail was falling from the sky. There was no
thunder, but the sky was rearranged every so often by a
lightening strike.

I often wonder about the times in my life when my
spiritual experiences have seemed like lightening — an
absolutely huge experience that fills my life with light for
only a flash and then disappears again as quickly. You are
never the same after experiencing that particular flash of
light. It's as if a part of your mind, body, and soul, is
awakened to a new knowledge, and that part of you can
never walk in darkness again.

The first time I had this type of experience was when
I was five years old. I of course had no awareness at that
time that I was experiencing a life-changing choice. I
only realized that later, when I looked back on the adventure. My whole family had gone to Herman Lake outside of Bonners Ferry, Idaho, for a swim. I remember my

brother Wynn, who was sixteen months older, being just as excited as I was. I had never been to Herman Lake, but playing in the water was just about as good as it could get in my 5-year-old opinion.

I was an extremely petite five-year-old and weighed about thirty pounds. When I was born I was a "pre-emie," having come into the world two months earlier than my parents or the doctors expected. In 1943 to weigh in at birth around three pounds and survive was pretty impressive. My brother and I had both been premature and the doctor had explained to my mother that both of us would probably be very slow, even re-tarded, as a result. My brother and I didn't know about this assessment of retardation, however, and we pro-ceeded to behave as if we were totally normal human beings, which for all intents and purposes we were and still are, at least academically speaking. My brother was my best friend and we agreed that the promise of swim-ming was just divine.

When we arrived at Herman Lake I was disap-pointed; it wasn't what I expected. We usually swam at lake Pend O'reille in Sandpoint, where there was a very sandy beach and shallow water. At Herman Lake there were little wooden dressing rooms, and Mom, Wynn and I all piled into one of them. There was no beach, just a drop off into the water. I was in such a hurry that I jumped out of my clothes, pulled on my suit and ran out the door as my mother called after me, "Wait for me!" I was ready to swim, and I didn't want to wait. I hit the water running. Immediately, I was in so deep that the water was over my head. I didn't know how to swim. I remember putting my hand up in the air as I would rise to the surface, and then I sank down again. Somewhere in my five-year-old mind I knew I had three chances of surfacing and going under before I would drown. I was not panicking. I wasn't afraid of dying. But as I went down for the second time, I recall asking for help from some higher source. I was going down for the third time, thinking I was dead, when I felt my little hand being grabbed by someone or something that then pulled me to the surface.

Choking and vomiting water, I was extracted from the depths of Herman Lake just as my mom came charging out of the dressing room. The lady who grabbed my hand later said she had noticed a little hand bobbing in out of the water and something made her decide to reach for it and pull whatever was attached to it out of the water. It was me. I remember being grateful, and thinking that I would have be more careful next time. As I look back on this incident, I think we are periodically given chances to exit from life if we choose to. At Herman Lake I had the opportunity to exit but decided I could deal with life in the human realm, and so I received assistance.

I never liked Herman Lake after that, but I still love the water. The majesty of a summer storm on Lake

Pend O'reille fills me with wonder. I've seen the waves on the north Idaho lake reach ten feet tall, as they crash against the beach. It has been said that water represents our human emotional body. Whenever we observe the bodies of water in our lives we should check out our emotions and see what's going on.

We are all connected to the energy of this planet, and when the emotions of many people get out of balance we can expect the waters of the planet to respond in like fashion. The lesson for me is to be responsible for my emotional body. It is truly a gift from God. Humans have an enormous capacity for joy and pain and a wide range of other emotions, perhaps greater than any species every created. How totally unique and magnificent we really are. Be aware of your emotions, don't repress them until they are forced to explode or flood. Examine them gently, honor them, pass them through your body, and then move on.

Slashing Clear-cuts
By Winston

In the sixties the Forest Service sold large acreages of timber to logging companies for the marketable timber that they contained. What was left were dead trees, trees too small or containing too much center-rot to be made into lumber. After the marketable timber was removed, either independent or Forest Service slashing crews used chain saws to fell all that was left standing. The area could then be burned clean after the first rains in the fall. The following spring these areas would be re-planted with marketable varieties of timber.

The summer after my logging accident (see Hit By a Tree) I went back to work for the Forest Service and again slashed clear-cuts. Looking back, I think of that summer as the most dangerous time of my life.

The job of clearing clear-cuts was put out for bid to independent contractors who bid by the acre. If a certain area did not receive any independent bids below the government- established maximum bid limit, they were slashed by Forest Service crews at an hourly rate that was considerably below the going rate for independent con- tractors. The independent contractors routinely overbid the established maximum for this particular area, which was about four hundred acres of predominately old- growth non-commercial cedar and hemlock that suffered from center-rot.

The reason that the job to clear-cut the Mission Creek area was overbid by independent contractors was that center-rot trees are dangerous and difficult to fall. Sometimes the only thing holding the big trees up in the air is a thin outer layer of wood and the bark. When you cut into a center-rot tree it can collapse into itself, splitting up the trunk and causing it to fall in a totally unpredictable manner. Some of these old-growth trees, most of them three to five feet in diameter, were just shells waiting to fall over and explode in all directions. My whole summer was spent dodging trees that might fall almost anyplace. I had one or two close calls a day. It was tremendously exciting then. I wouldn't dream of doing it now.

Sometimes a felled tree would hang up in another tree. The only safe way to deal with this situation was to cut another tree further upslope that would then hit the hung-up trees and knock all of them down like dominos. This created a tremendous noise as broken limbs and pieces of the trunk went flying everywhere when three or four big trees would crash into each other and tumble down the hillside. Alan, a crew member, held that summer's record for orchestrating the simultaneous knockdown of seven monster trees.

Wind was always a factor. An unexpected gust could change the direction the tree would fall. We were careful to saw all the brush from around the base so we could get away from any tree that might fall unpredictably.

Forest Service crews were also on call to fight fires. One Friday, after working all day, we were ordered to a fire. Since I had experience with chainsaws, my responsibility was to cut logs and roots to help establish a nonburnable fire line. I also felled any snags that could reach workers on the fire line.

Early that next morning I volunteered to cut a particularly dangerous tree. This tree had been burning most of the night and was endangering people working on the fire line. The area around the base of the tree was on fire so I cut and carried green poles to stand on while I was cutting. It was still dark, and smoke was swirling in such a fashion as to make it difficult to determine the natural lean of the tree. I had a helper whose job was to stand behind me, hold my belt, and look up for falling pieces of wood while I worked. He would yank me out of the way if any big chunks of burning wood started falling from the tree. This particular time, almost everything that could happen, did happen. A two-hundred pound, fire-sharpened spear of tree trunk almost impaled me, but my helper yanked me away at the last moment. The chainsaw I was working with caught on fire and had to be put out with shoveled dirt, and my boots almost caught on fire because the green poles I was standing on had started to burn. After I got that tree down I thanked my helper for keeping me out of harm's way. I still have flashbacks about that particular incident.

Today I wonder why I performed those tasks with

such positive enthusiasm. I could have been killed on any given day because close calls happened several times a day. Years later I went to the movie "Sometimes a Great Notion" with Paul Newman and Henry Fonda. The logging accidents portrayed in the movie were accurate renditions of a reality I was very familiar with. Watching that movie I was more uncomfortable than I would have been in any horror or suspense movie, because I knew what was going to happen next.

Logging is a hazardous profession. Most of the worst accidents that happened in the movie I had somehow avoided. I don't think it was all youth and fast reflexes; Looking back, I'm sure I was protected. I don't necessarily know why. Grace, I guess.

Hit by a Tree
By Winston

At the end of spring semester 1964 I went to work for the Moyie River Lumber Company as a choker setter. Choker setting is one of the most dangerous jobs in the woods because it is where the most inexperienced workers start out. All the heavy machinery such as bulldozers, trucks, loaders, and chainsaws made so much noise that the sound of breaking wood, which was a warning alarm for old-time axe and cross-cut loggers, was completely drowned out. Gill pokes (sticks and small trees), poked into, around, and through the roll cage of the cat where I rode on the toolbox. One-hundred percent vigilance was vital. Freak accidents could happen at any time.

I had been working for the Forest Service during previous summers and I wanted to make more money and try something more exciting. I knew it was more dangerous, but I was young and quick, and I believed I was strong enough to avoid any dangers that would come my way. I was treated well by the crew even though I was a college boy. Everyone knew my father and had done business with him by buying appliances, televisions, or chain saws. I was the most inexperienced man on the crew but I had a reputation for being a good worker.

My job was to sit on the bulldozer's metal tool chest to the right of the cat skinner (the driver) and pull the fifteen-foot, one-inch diameter steel wire chokers (cables) off the hooks on the back of the roll cage where they were stored. Then I would jump off the cat, put the choker around a log, hook it's bell, and attach the choker to the bull-line hook on the back of the cat. Initially, the cat skinner, a wiry man in his forties, could do his job of driving the cat and hooking logs much faster than I could, but gradually I learned to work with the steel wire chokers rather than fight them. It was an exhausting job but I reveled in intense excitement of dodging gill pokes coming into the roll cage, or jumping out of the way of logs that suddenly started rolling my direction because of the earth shaking vibrations of the heavy equipment and falling trees. It was a thrill a minute.

One day three weeks into the summer, I was riding on my seat on the tool chest when the cat stopped. I jumped up from my seat on the toolbox and reached for a choker when the three-foot diameter, twenty-five-foot tall snag we had just rounded fell because of the vibration of our passing. It hit me with a glancing blow and smashed into the toolbox where I had been sitting seconds before. If I had been any slower I would have been crushed. As it was, I fell five or six feet to the ground and landed on my back. I remember looking up at blue sky and clouds and feeling terrible pain. I got up and found that I could still move, but then I collapsed to the ground again in pain.

Men came from everywhere and carried me to a pickup. Someone drove me over twenty miles of rough, chuck-holed gravel road and thirty miles of highway to the Bonners Ferry Community Hospital. In the emergency room our family doctor started cleaning my wounds. He was angry and didn't hide his attitude about logging jobs. "Why someone like you, who has the opportunity to get an education, took a job like that, I just don't know. Those jobs are for people who can't do anything else." As he treated me he was not his normal gentle self. He assessed the damage and told me that all the muscles in my back were severely bruised. No bones were broken but I was not able stand or walk without pain for months.

I spent the rest of the summer lying around. After a month I was able to stay by myself at our cabin on Lake Pend O'reille and swim three or four times a day. Floating in the water relieved the pain and so swimming became my physical therapy. I swam a mile or so a day even though I couldn't stand or walk well. It was December before I was pain-free. My parents paid for my next year's education because needless to say I hadn't earned any money. Back in school, happy to have those lost six months behind me, I was unaware of how the accident would eventually shape my future.

Two years later, in spring semester 1966, I was about to graduate. In addition to receiving a vocal performance Bachelor's degree, I had earned a music education certification just in case I might decide to teach music someday. My plans were to be a performer, or to teach in college, but I had been going to school for six years and I wanted a break. As soon as I graduated in late May my II S military deferment would change and I would be eligible for the draft. I decided to go into the military, get a commission, serve a term, and use G.I Bill benefits to go to graduate school. The Marine Corps was on campus and I took their officer candidate test, passed the physical, was accepted, and was slated to go to Quantico, Virginia shortly after graduation.

In 1966, Vietnam was not a big part of the news. I did not put great stock in the possibility that I could be killed, maimed, or psychologically marred for life. Almost twenty-four, I had just started going out with Roberta, whom I liked a lot. But since I was going into the Marines almost immediately after graduation, I didn't foresee that we'd develop a serious relationship. I was focused on running and doing push-ups and getting into shape so as not to be washed out of the program. The Marines sent me letters regularly about their schedule and expectations. I was excited about accepting the challenge.

Because a report of my logging accident was included in my medical history, I was ordered to report to the orthopedic specialist at Fairchild Air Force base in Spokane for an examination. It turned out that although my back had completely healed, the deformed, extra vertebra they found in my lower back washed me out of the program. As the middle-aged orthopedic specialist put it: "Son, you are not going into the military. Count yourself lucky and have a good life." At first I was disappointed. I had been getting ready to accept a new challenge. What would I do now? Those nine student-teaching credits all of a sudden assumed new importance. I decided to find a teaching job for a couple of years and then go to graduate school. My relationship with Roberta became a lot more important; we were engaged by June. A music-teaching job opened in Moscow and I was hired. I was lucky that the position had become available, and more so that as a first-year teacher in a competitive market in a university town, I was chosen to fill it.

Had I gone to the Marines, I would have graduated from OCS in December of 1966. My first assignment would probably have been Vietnam. Looking back, I know that I would have been a good soldier for a while. I could snap-shoot birds and deer off the end of the barrel. If I had been confronted by a fourteen-year-old holding a weapon pointed at me, I would have shot. I would also have regretted it for the rest of my life. I killed two deer in my hunting days and I regret it still. I did not enjoy eating those animals. Killing people would have altered me in ways I don't want to even imagine.

That accident with the snag caused the examination which found the congenital vertebrae which kept me from going to Vietnam. I don't think it was a random accident. I still have occasional flashbacks. I relive the moment immediately after being hit. I am lying on my back, wondering if my back is broken, looking at the blue sky with clouds. A moment earlier I had been sitting right where the snag hit. If I had moved a second slower, I would be dead. It is a chilling thought. Somehow, I was spared.

Trial by Fire
By Dolora

It is New Years Eve of 2001. Amazing changes have taken place this year. My Uncle Cliff is in the process of leaving his physical body behind. He has requested that we do not come watch him die. I readily agree for he has always been a source of love for me. The most memorable event occurred in January of 1962.

It truly was the proverbial "dark and stormy night" in north Idaho. The temperature was about ten degrees Fahrenheit outside, the winter wind was roaring viciously around the corners of our house in the country. Some problem had caused the power to go out and I was reduced to doing my homework by candlelight. My Dad was in Spokane, Washington, on business, my older brother was away at college, and Mom was somewhere in town. It was about 10:30 PM and Mom had called to say she would soon be on her way home. She told me to make sure to put out the fire in the fireplace and dump the ashes down the ash pit if I went to bed before she arrived home.

I finished my homework, put out the fire, and was headed for bed when I glanced at my watch. It was after midnight and Mom still wasn't home. I started to worry because we lived on top of a hill with no guardrails on the side of the road. It was a steep drop off to the valley below. My imagination started running wild with visions of Mom sliding off the icy roads over the cliff. I started calling all of Mom's friends to see if she was at their house.

Finally, I tracked her down still visiting with the minister of our church. She had lost track of time. I read her the riot act about not communicating and coming home on time. She apologized and said she would be home immediately. Minutes later she walked in the door and we both headed for bed in our cold house just as the power was restored.

I set my alarm clock for 6:30 AM and fell sound asleep. Startled by the buzzing of the alarm clock, I was jarred out of a sound slumber. My clock read 6:00 AM. I wrestled with the idea of turning over and grabbing another 30 minutes of sleep, but something made me decide to get up. Stumbling to the bathroom, I started pulling the curlers out of my hair. I could smell smoke! I followed the smell into family room where all around the base of the fireplace hearth smoke was seeping up from the basement. I threw open the basement door and called to my dog Mitzi, who slept in the basement. She let out only one bark. Smoke poured up from the basement and filled the kitchen. I yelled to my mother, "Mom, get up! Our house is on fire!"

She answered, "Let it burn."

My next instinct was to call the fire department. "Please help us, our house is on fire!" I gave them my location.

The dispatcher answered, "I'm sorry you're out of city limits. Try the Forest Service, maybe they can help you."

I called the Forest Service who replied, "We could have someone there in about three hours."

I hung up. What could I do now? "Mom! please get out of bed!" I yelled again. This time she got up.

The temperature had fallen to zero degrees Fahrenheit. My eighty-year-old grandfather lived next door, but I didn't think he could help. I knew my Uncle Cliff would help me so I tore across the street to his house in my pajamas, my bare feet sticking to the ice. I burst through his door screaming, "Uncle Cliff! Come help me! My house is on fire and no one will come!" He rose up from a deep sleep, pulled on his clothes in seconds, laced up heavy logging boots and was at my house in a matter of minutes.

Cliff surveyed the problem. There were no flames upstairs, only smoke coming from the basement. He called Mitzi and got her to come upstairs. Slowly he slid down the basement stairs on his stomach, trying to keep as low as possible so that he could breathe. In the basement there was a water faucet with a hose hooked to it. He found the source of the fire, the wood box underneath the ash pit, and doused the flames.

It seems the contractor who had put in the fireplace and ash pit had installed a wooden bottom in the ash container. The hot ashes had burned through the bottom and then into the basement wood box, which was located directly under the ash pit. Uncle Cliff put out the fire in the wood box before it could burn the rest of the house, but the smoke damage was intense. The whole house had to be cleaned and repainted. All our furniture, drapes, and clothes had to be cleaned.

My Uncle saved our house with no thought for his own safety. As I reflect back on this incident in my life, I ask myself, What was the lesson? I know that some force caused my alarm clock to go off early, and that same force provided assistance in the form of my Uncle Cliff when no other source was available.

As my Uncle Cliff is in the process of dying, I know that he was a human acting with angelic power at the time of the fire. It is my prayer that as he transcends this physical realm that he does it with the peace and knowingness that he is not alone. My trial by fire only turned out to be a need to clear the smoke so that I could see with clarity that I was always provided for and protected.

****

My Uncle Cliff released his body three days after I wrote this story. I am told he was peaceful and there was a smile on his face.

Asleep at the Wheel
By Winston

Spring 1966. It was in my last year as an undergraduate at the University of Idaho. My schedule included taking nine credits of student teaching, singing the title role of Puccini's "Gianni Schicchi" for opera theater, playing the French horn with the wind ensemble and orchestra, singing and soloing with the Vandaleer traveling choir, and maintaining a good grade point average. I had just started dating a girl I had known for four years and she seemed to be the best choice of girls I had dated so far. I had never been so busy before.

For the first time I was forced to draw up a schedule which included all my classes, an hourly commute each way to Lewiston to practice teach for half a day three days a week, applied music classes in voice, opera theater, orchestra and wind ensemble, practice times for voice and French horn, music education classes, dates with my new girlfriend, and ten or fifteen hours a week of work at the Student Union. I had also planned sleep time from 11:00 PM until 6:00 AM and a nap from 5:15 PM until 6:00 PM. It was a rigorous schedule but I was serious about keeping it. It worked beyond all of my expectations.

In winter the road to Lewiston was much more difficult than it is now. The trip down and up the grade had more curves, less turnouts and passing lanes, and it was longer. A fellow music education major shared the ride and gasoline. I drove.

One day early in March we were coming back from Lewiston in early afternoon. The grade had been clear but wet. On top at the higher elevation there were patches of slush, but we got through it. I heaved a sigh of relief. My fellow teacher was sleeping, the sun was shining, and the bad road was behind us. It was warm in the car, and my concentration drifted. I must have fallen asleep. I awoke suddenly when the car drifted into the slush on the shoulder. We were heading directly for a four-foot metal road marker. Stomping on the brakes could send us sideways or throw us into the ditch or cause a rollover, not that I thought about it. I pumped the brakes gently, and as we slammed into the road marker the sheet metal top broke off and sliced through the windshield at eye level. Why it stopped half way through, and didn't slice one of us through the head, has always been a mystery to me. Scientifically, one could say that the force of the impact just was not quite big enough for the sheet metal to make it all the way into the car and through our heads. The rest of the windshield was not cracked or broken. There was only a horizontal slot, the exact same gauge as the metal, cut into it.

The impact had startled my passenger awake. I got out and pulled the metal out of the windshield. We backed off the post, which had put a small dent in the hood before it bent under the car, and drove the rest of the way to Moscow, feeling lucky and not talking much. My student teacher friend told me the next day his wife wasn't comfortable with him riding with me. I told him I would try to get more sleep before Lewiston teaching days.

The semester proved to be very special. Besides getting an A in student teaching I received A's in all my classes. It was my first four-point semester. My solo performances all went well. As the semester progressed so also did my relationship with Roberta. I started looking for jobs in eastern Washington because they paid more, but I really wanted to stay as close as possible because I knew I would be spending most weekends in Moscow.

A vocal music position in Moscow opened in April and I applied for the job. For a first-year teacher to get a job teaching music in a University town was almost unheard of. Roberta and I got engaged in June and I taught vocal music at the junior and senior high for the next two years assisting with the orchestra and band programs. It was a perfect first job that gave me a great variety of experience. After two years, we moved to Seattle where I had been accepted into the University of Washington graduate school with a small scholarship.

Looking back I see a pattern of protection and guidance that to me is way beyond luck or circumstance.

Bashed by a Buick

By Winston

On June 15, 1985, I was riding my bicycle to my new job at Tracor Aerospace in Austin, Texas. I had been working in construction, building houses in the hills west of town. Working in residential construction had allowed me to come and go so I was available to take any short-term singing "gigs." But I had become disenchanted with performing and I wanted to try something other than music. Our next door neighbor, Jim Lewis, had been working for Tracor for years and suggested that my liberal arts education would allow me to come in at entry level at about the same money I was making as a framer plus benefits, something I didn't have in construction. The plant was only two miles away. I was in good shape from building houses so I figured the ride would be less than fifteen minutes to work.

I pulled onto the almost empty four-lane wide street that led downhill to the plant and started shifting into higher gears to take advantage of the downhill grade. I heard the sound of a car directly behind me and felt my bicycle surge forward and off the paved road into the gravel and down the embankment. My left leg hurt. I looked around and no one was on the road. I looked at my leg. It was not pretty. I figured out later that a car or something had hit the axle of my bicycle's rear wheel and suddenly accelerated me to the speed of the car. The metal toe clip on the pedal whipped around and peeled the skin and fat layer off the calf of my left leg. When I went off the road and fell from my bicycle, the skin flap opened and my leg was dragged through the gravel, sticks, dirt, and ants of the embankment. My leg felt as if a baseball bat had whacked it at full force. The open cut was full of dirt and debris. I rose up and saw a car coming up the road. I screamed for help, and they stopped. I asked them to go to my house and tell Roberta what had happened, and to call an ambulance.

Three firemen were on the scene within a few minutes. I remember looking up into the face of one of them as he grabbed my shoulders and started dragging me up the embankment and toward the road. The pain he caused my already injured body was almost intolerable, I asked him a one-word question, "Why?" When he replied, "Snakes," I found new resources of pain control.

The ambulance and my wife arrived about the same time. I don't remember much about the trip except that it seemed to take a long time to travel five miles. At the hospital the emergency room staff turned me on my stomach and started cleaning the wound on my leg. They would not administer any serious pain medication because the bumps and scratches on my head indicated a possible concussion.

As I lay on my stomach on a wet metal cart, people worked on my leg with tweezers and saline solution. I tried to control my breathing with the yoga exercises I had learned related to my singing. Roberta and I reversed the roles of coach and subject that we had learned for her pregnancy. At one point a doctor came by and suggested to the attending people that Roberta should go to the waiting room. Though the nurses had originally been skeptical about the yoga procedures, they responded by telling him that my blood pressure and vital signs were remarkably close to normal in spite of my injuries. From this point on the yoga techniques were viewed more positively, and the doctor made it official that Roberta could stay. We sustained this process for four hours with no pain medication other than topical. Sometime around noon the emergency staff decided that I didn't have a concussion and I could go to the operating room where they could give me a general anesthetic and work on me in earnest.

When I awoke I was told I would be in traction with my leg elevated for approximately ten days to allow the swelling to go down to allow for a skin graft. My immediate supervisor at Tracor came to my room in person to inform me that I was in his prayers and that my job would be waiting for me when I could come back.

Roberta and I didn't have medical insurance. This accident was a hit-and-run, so we didn't know the insurance company of the other person(s) involved or their names. I had only worked for Tracor Aerospace for two days and so I didn't yet qualify for their medical insurance. It looked like I wouldn't be working for weeks. Roberta reported the hit-and-run accident to police. She and our friend and neighbor, Jim Lewis, searched the accident site and found a passenger-side, rearview mirror that looked as of it had recently been knocked off a car. Further investigation indicated it had come from a middle-to late-seventies GM car, probably a Buick. Jim and Roberta went so far as to stand by the road at the same time of day and watch for cars matching the paint color and missing a right-side rearview mirror. Within two days they saw a car missing a passenger-side mirror, recorded the license number, and turned it over to police. When the police found the car the mirror's color and bent screw holes matched the Buick perfectly. The driver, who didn't have any insurance, claimed he didn't know he'd hit anyone. Our hopes were dashed. How would we pay all the expenses?

Roberta called our car insurance agency to see if there was any provision for being on a bicycle and being hit by a car. The local agent said they could pay up to $2500. The hospital and doctor bills at the end of the third day were around $9,000. Someone suggested to Roberta that she call the State of Texas insurance office and ask about our situation. They told her to read our policy carefully to see if we had an uninsured-motorist clause, in which case we would be covered to the full extent of our per-person liability coverage, which was $25,000.

I vaguely remembered our car insurance salesman

suggesting we purchase an add-on rider, which only cost a few extra dollars a month. We had reluctantly decided it was something we should probably do. When Roberta called our insurance company a representative told her that their coverage didn't apply to bicycle riders. Roberta called the State of Texas Insurance office again and they not only suggested that a standard clause regarding "intentional accidents" might also apply, they called our insurance company and told them we had coverage amounting to $27,500.

Had Roberta and Jim Lewis not done the detective work to find the mirror and the license number of the Buick, had we not had the add-on uninsured rider in our policy, had Roberta not been told to call the state office and then called them back, we would have had to pay most of the expenses.

I returned to work on crutches in six weeks, progressed to a cane, and by late September was walking normally without pain. I have a really ugly scar, and the muscle twitches continuously, but I can run, walk, and do everything I want physically.

There were a lot of coincidences involved with this accident. If the car had been driving an inch to the left, it would have hit my leg directly. If it had been driving an inch to the right, it would have collapsed the rear wheel. Either impact could have thrown me in front of the car and killed or seriously injured me; instead, I was knocked away from the car. Doctors were concerned about the possibility of permanent toe drop; I walk perfectly. Roberta, by being very assertive, "found" the money to pay all medical bills plus an excess of $13, 000 for pain and suffering. I don't know why this happened, but I was cared for in many ways. I shudder when I think of how much worse it could have been. It took me five years to get on a bicycle again. I am not comfortable riding in traffic although I do like mountain biking.

The human body, tough and resilient though it may be, is no match for an automobile going fifty or sixty miles an hour. The human spirit, on the other hand probably has no limits. During this time I prayed for healing, as did Frank Akins, my Tracor supervisor. His church and my family included me on their prayer lists. I sang at Frank's church several times afterwards and have maintained our friendship. My requests for healing all were granted.

I participated in a civil suit against the driver of the car by our insurance company two years later. In that time the police department had lost the Buick rearview mirror from their locked storage, the driver no longer had the car, and pictures taken at the time showing the match of the mirror to the car were not convincing to the jury. The jury felt I shouldn't have been riding a bicycle to work even though local bicycle racers trained there regularly. They awarded damages of one dollar to the driver. He declared bankruptcy immediately after the trial because he couldn't afford to pay his lawyer.

Except for my pain and suffering, the driver's lawyer and our insurance provider were the real victims.

Everyone seems to have some pain and suffering in their lives, it makes the sweetness sweeter. It also teaches compassion.

Broadway Exit
By Dolora

Christmas time in December of 1996 was imminent. I was anxiously awaiting the arrival of our daughter and son. Wendy was finishing college and Ryan was working at the Board of Trade in Chicago. It seems that Christmas was the only time we could all arrange to be in each other's lives physically, and I really loved it when skiing together was the day's agenda. Sun Valley, Idaho, is a fairyland during the Christmas season with all the white twinkling lights and pristine snow. It's almost impossible to not be seduced by the beauty of the season whether you are visiting or you live there all year round.

Wendy was a junior at Northern Arizona State University in Flagstaff. Relationship issues were plaguing her. She had decided to leave the situation she was in and change schools for the third time. Academics had never been a problem for Wendy. Her challenges came in other arenas of life.

Just before New Year's, Wendy flew back to Flagstaff and packed up her belongings, which for a college student at that time were considerable. I flew to Flagstaff — 2-inch packing tape and black permanent marker in hand — to help her address boxes and tape them up, all 50 of them. With this done, we patiently awaited the arrival of UPS to pick-up the boxes from the garage and give us the freedom to continue on our journey.

Early the next morning, we bid our good byes and headed for Sun Valley. Wendy owned a little red Volkswagen convertible, which was great for Flagstaff, but not necessarily wonderful for snow country. This car was loaded to the gills with almost no room to put a purse, let alone the nightshirt I had brought along for the trip. Wendy's knees were under her chin as she drove, in order to make room for all the things in the back seat too precious or awkward to ship. The winter weather was being particularly kind, the sun was shining although the landscape around Flagstaff was dotted with patches of snow.

I was glad to have some time with my daughter to see how she really was doing after all. Breaking up is hard to do. Wendy and I talked; the journey was crowded with emotions and memories of her time in Flagstaff. The trip took on a flavor of nostalgia as we passed from mountains to desert to mountains and canyons. All the emotions being shared were represented in the variety of the landscape; we truly went from highs to lows to emptiness. We drove hard and as dusk started to descend we decided to stay in a little town on the edge of Bryce Canyon in Utah.

Early the next morning we continued our journey, trying to stay in front of the storms that were building. We were pushing to get home and I took my turn at driving the little red convertible with my knees under my chin on into Salt Lake. It had started snowing and

Wendy and I changed driving responsibilities. I kept asking the angels to keep our path clear and sunny. Sun Valley appeared over the horizon without incident.

Wendy started researching universities to see which ones started late enough in January so she would not miss a semester of school. The University of Montana in Missoula didn't start until the 25th of January. She applied and was immediately accepted. We headed for Missoula to find her a place to live. At mid-year the housing choices were slim, but it was important to find a place we could afford that was not a dump. We toured the offices of property management companies and cruised the newspapers knowing we would be guided to the perfect place.

It appeared, that perfect place, 2001 Lester Street, a little one-bedroom house with a garage for the convertible. How lucky could we be? We headed back to the property management company, who informed us that the house had already been rented. Somewhat defeated, but knowing that life is always in "Divine Order," Wendy and I decided that if she was to finish her education in Missoula the house would become available for her in time to start the semester.

We had been fortunate in our timing, as the weatherman's forecast of no snow was actually accurate. The two of us started the six-hour journey back to Sun Valley, having left our appropriate phone numbers with the property management company, in case there was any change in the rental status of the little house on Lester.

We arrived home to the vision of the answering machine blinking with a single important message, "The house on Lester is yours, please send a $500 deposit."

There are no accidents. Angelic assistance had provided a home for Wendy's heart and soul to grow and be nurtured.

My body was growing very tired of running, packing and traveling. All of this activity had taken place in about two weeks time, but there was just one more trip to make. Bless the grandparents in Boise, who had stored some of Wendy's belongings when she attended Boise State University. Our next trip was to Boise to pack up and retrieve a king-size bed and some chairs that had been stashed at Grandpa Deal's. (Please don't ask what a college student is doing with a king-size bed to move and store because it is a long story and not pertinent to this particular adventure.)

Permanent marker in hand, Wendy and I boxed and labeled all the possessions left in Boise, sending them on their way to the little yellow house on Lester Street, Missoula, Montana. I was exhausted and I knew I was pushing my energy reserves.

The January weather was still holding, it was 5:00 PM and we were finally headed home. I totally trusted my little white Ford Explorer. I entered rush-hour traffic on the freeway and slowly applied my foot to the accelerator as I started up a slight incline.

Without any warning, the car started spinning 360-degree circles on black ice. Traffic was coming at me fast. I hit the guardrail on one side then spun again and hit the guardrail on the other side. I remember thinking that we were going to die. That didn't seem to concern me, however, because a calmness settled over me, and I never hit the brakes in panic. When we finally stopped spinning, we were facing all the five o'clock traffic coming straight at us. It flowed around us effortlessly, however, and somehow I managed to get out of the car and check the damage. Wendy and I were fine, but the car was not. I pulled the rear fender out and away from the tire and found out that the Explorer could still run. We were still facing the oncoming traffic, but off to the left was a little steep hill. By gently easing down a makeshift trail, I accessed the freeway going back into Boise, back to Grandpa's house. I thanked the angels for keeping us safe.

Shaking, I called my husband Steve and informed him of our dilemma and that we would not be home that evening. I wasn't aware of the many miracles taking place that day, only that we had survived rush-hour traffic without being killed. The steel frame for the king-size bed was in the Explorer. It had not been strapped down and it had broken the visor above my daughter's head, yet had left her untouched.

My husband had a wonderful friend who managed a

rental-car agency and he delivered a car directly to the auto body shop where the Explorer was to be repaired. We transferred all the items that were bound for Lester Street, the sun was shining once again, and soon we headed home for Sun Valley.

The lesson I learned from this experience was, don't drive yourself to the point of exhaustion. I truly believe that sickness and accidents can occur only at certain frequencies, and if you keep yourself out of those lower frequencies you can avoid many hardships. I also learned that it didn't matter which direction I was going, I was totally protected by angels because I always ask for their protection. The first rule of angelic intervention is, you must ask.

Feathers, Fur, and Nature

My life has always been blessed by nature. I have been employed in the veterinary field for many years and acceptance from animals and nature, when it is mirrored back to you, helps you to accept yourself. I am so grateful. Dolora

The world around us is a source of inspiration and beauty. It also provides us with guides and experiences that teach us lessons. Winston

Papers and Protection
By Dolora

The sun had finished its journey from the other side of the world and had just arrived to kiss the north Idaho Mountain tops. The rays of sun triggered my alarm clock. Six AM time to get up, sixty dailies to deliver. The Spokesman Review was always on time. My brother Wynn and I split the paper route. He took the thirty papers to the south and I delivered the thirty papers to the north. We had followed the same routine for two years.

Hat, coat, and gloves donned, I slung my white canvas paper bag over my shoulder, counted out thirty dailies, and headed for Dr. Elliss' house next door. Mitzi, my little blond cocker Spaniel, always went with me. She knew all the dogs on the route and was greeted with tail wags at every location. I was eleven years old and I truly didn't mind the paper route. My father was always a believer that hard work built character, so, my character got built three hundred and sixty-five days a year. At that time in the morning no one was up to interrupt your thoughts or tell you what you should think. I loved hearing the birds and watching the sun change the landscape as it progressed over the mountains. I truly connected with all the dogs on my route and I greeted each of them by name as Mitzi and I arrived to bring the daily news.

As Mitzi and I traveled from house to house we would collect the dog that lived there to help us continue on our journey. I didn't think anything of it at the time because it seemed like a natural occurrence. The Toutfist's house was next, then Buhler's and on to Frederickson's. By this time I had three dogs in my entourage. The Pace house appeared and I always tried to put the paper on the porch so that the paper stayed dry. These were old people and I knew they had trouble getting around. I would even put the paper inside the screen door whenever possible so that all they had to do was open their door. I headed for Banker's Street, so named by the children of Bonners Ferry. Mr. McNally, the banker, had an imposing house that stood at the end of the street. It was one of the few paved streets in the small town and everyone who lived there was considered upper crust.

By this time I was accompanied by a gaggle of thir-teen dogs, all getting along running and playing with each other. This seemed natural to me because it hap-pened every morning. No dogfights occurred and all the dogs left my papers where I placed them. No one misbe-haved by digging or pooping inappropriately. I loved the dogs. They made me feel safe, especially in winter when it was dark and I delivered papers before the sun ever arrived.

On that particular morning the sun was with us, the leaves had just begun falling from the trees. Banker's

Street had a lot of maple trees with really good leaves that crackled when you walked in them. You could kick leaves from house to house. I enjoyed the fall, particularly on Banker's Street. However, this morning the dogs were tense. They kept sticking close to me, not running or barking, and they were actually under my feet. I was almost at the end of Banker's Street, which was on the hill above the railroad tracks. Sometimes, if you took a shortcut to town, down the hillside, you would come across a hobo's camp by the railroad. If we took this route, which was the fastest way into town, my brother and I often stumbled over a smoldering campfire the hobos had built.

I was at my last house when I looked up because the dogs had started barking uproariously. Across the street from me was a stranger. He was dirty and I knew he was from the hobo's camp down below. What was he doing in this neighborhood? I never saw anybody on my route. He just stood there and stared at me. The longer he stared and stood the more the dogs barked. It was not their usually friendly greeting. They sounded vicious. All thirteen dogs had gathered around me like a train of wagons waiting for the Indian attack. I felt totally safe. No one could have gotten within twenty feet of me and not been charged by my four-legged cavalry. All the doors of the houses started swinging open. People in their robes and pajamas wanted to see what the ruckus was about. Everyone asked me if I was okay. I replied in the affirmative as I continued down the street delivering the last of my papers.

I arrived safely at home; all my dog soldiers had dispersed themselves back to their homes to enjoy breakfast. From that point in my life I lost all fear of the dark or being alone. I was protected by a force so loving that I knew I could always count on being safe. Protection comes in many forms, but love is the greatest.

Scraggles the Cat
By Winston

We had moved to the White Salmon, Washington, area from Boise after living with Roberta's parents for a year. I had been working in construction and doing some substitute teaching in the area and Roberta was teaching elementary music half time at the middle school in White Salmon. While we lived in Texas, our Washington teaching certificates had been grandfathered into lifetime certificates. This enabled both of us to teach without picking up credits, clock hours, or jumping through any academic hoops.

Scraggles the cat came to us in a zero-weather February while we were living in a trailer park in B-Z Corners, Washington. We had had cats before that we had picked from litters or the pound. Jack the cat had come with us from Texas. We didn't want or need another kitty, but late in the fall we had noticed a longhaired, brown, tabby who seemed to have been dumped by someone, or was a runaway. The cat was unapproachable and would sometimes attack Roberta on her way to or from the woodpile. As the winter progressed, the cat's fur became more matted and he seemed too skinny to survive. By February, it became apparent that he was living in the crawl space under our rented trailer. The manager of the trailer park wasn't particular fastidious about maintenance; I had been under the trailer to repair some plumbing, and it was not a nice place.

When the temperature dropped into the teens, I started leaving some dry cat food on the porch. It always disappeared overnight. Later in the month the weather forecast was for temperatures below zero. I opened the door to put some food on the porch and the cat was there waiting. I didn't feel right about leaving him outside. I asked him if he wanted to spend the night inside since it was so cold. I placed the bowl of food just inside the door and the cat came inside. He ate his fill and went to the space under the wood stove and pro-ceeded to soak up as much heat as he could. Jack hated the intruder, but kept his distance. I can't remember when I named him Scraggles; it seemed to fit his be-draggled, matted, fur and unpredictable nature. Except in nice weather, when he sometimes likes to stay outside, Scraggles has slept inside ever since.

Scraggles was still untouchable, but gradually I could give him one or two strokes when I put his dish of food in front of him. He would start to purr immediately upon being touched and then after a stroke or two would slash with his claws or bite with his teeth. Roberta suggested we take him to the pound. He was not a nice cat and we had Jack. He shed longhaired fur, was mean, and didn't seem to have any redemptive value. I pointed out that no one would adopt Scraggles; he was a sure bet to be euthanized.

One day I was reading when I realized that Scraggles

was sitting behind me with one paw lightly touching my shoulder. Gradually, over several months, I could pet and hold him for longer lengths of time. He trained me to stop any demonstration of physical affection just short of his tolerance limit. He didn't seem to know how to accept love; his petting threshold became overloaded easily. He seemed to not be threatened by touching me lightly with one paw and he loved soaking up heat under the wood stove. We feared that he would spontaneously combust because his fur would get so hot.

I think accepting the challenge to take on the taming of Scraggles was inspired by the example of my Grandpa Howard's feral cat, Minnie Pearl, who had come to him from the wild to join the circle of barn cats that attended morning and evening milking sessions. I have a picture in my mind of those cats from my childhood waiting patiently to be squirted in the face with hot milk straight from the cow. Grandpa's aim was flawless, he could squirt cat or kid at will, producing gales of laughter from the kids. The cats loved it, too. Minnie Pearl became grandpa's cat; she lived in the woods but lounged on his lap when he listened to the radio. No one else could touch Minnie Pearl.

Scraggles became a metaphor for our teaching. We both have had students who didn't know how to respond to kindness and love because of their background. They had to learn over time to trust that we would be constant. It was painful for them and us. Perseverance in affection, although sometimes seemingly impossible, is an incredibly strong force.

Scraggles is still not quite tame; he has been with my mother since my father died three years ago. He is healthy for his age and he is helping to train my two-year-old son. My mother has broken him of sleeping on her chest at night. She accuses me of spoiling that cat.

Ryan's Black Baron
By Dolora

As good parents, we all try to teach our children responsibility. One of the ways we do this is by giving them a pet to love and care for, and we were no exception to the process.

When Ryan was ten years old he wanted a dog in the worst way, and a black Labrador was his choice. My husband researched kennels in the Seattle area to find a good line of Labs, not a blockheaded show-type but a compact, strong, hunting dog. He found a kennel he liked and when there was a litter of pups we traveled to Everett, Washington, to pick up our seven-week-old puppy.

Ryan went into the kennel and one of the puppies chose him. We wrote out the check, piled back into the suburban, and headed back to the ferry to take our new responsibility home. Baron, as he was so christened, nestled into the back seat beside Ryan, never fussing or making a peep. We set up the baby playpen right next to Ryan's bed so that Baron could be with him all night. We had expected the usual first-night-away-from-the-litter problems but we were not prepared for the lengthy separation anxiety this puppy would suffer.

He started to cry, so Ryan curled up and slept with him. He still cried. The prescribed puppy comfort treatments, from a radio, to old clothes of Ryan's, to an alarm clock, all proved unsuccessful. Two weeks later the puppy was still crying all night long. Ryan had become sick from lack of sleep, so in desperation I took the puppy out of Ryan's room. So much for teaching your child responsibility, I thought. I settled into the rocking lounge chair in the living room, placed the puppy on my chest, covered us both with a blanket, and lo and behold, peace took over. For the first time in two weeks the household slept.

Ryan and Baron grew up together learning from each other. Ryan even taught Baron to ride on a Ski-Doo with him on Payette Lake in McCall, Idaho. Such was Baron's trust in Ryan that he would do anything Ryan asked.

As Baron matured he sensed his role in the family was that of comedian. After we moved to Sun Valley, Idaho, Baron lived in the house full time instead of in his kennel. When things were tense at work or in the family, Baron would run to the laundry basket, search out underwear, and run to the living room with it in his mouth, especially if there were guests. His best trick was lying on his back throwing underwear into the air and catching it with his front paws. If he wasn't tossing someone's drawers, he would grab towels out of the bathroom and proceed to demonstrate his throwing and catching ability. He only did this when he sensed that someone needed cheering up. He knew that oftentimes laughter is the relief button.

Baron was definitely more intelligent than your average dog. If you mentioned the word WORK or BALL in his presence he would start spinning in circles. He loved going to work because he was truly a "car dog" from the first ride of his life. He would race to the car, anxiously dance until he was permitted to jump in, then turn around three times, lie down, and become invisible.

Not a peep would be heard from until it was time to get out. He would go to work and patiently wait in the car all day with his bowl of water just to have a ride. His passion for riding was only exceeded by his passion for retrieving balls and sticks. Baron was so in tune with the words BALL and WORK that we started spelling them in his presence just to keep his living room antics down to a minimum. Wouldn't you know it, Baron learned to spell.

Ryan graduated from high school, worked that summer, kissed his beloved dog good-bye and headed for college. Baron moved his sleeping quarters to the end of my bed when Ryan departed, and I became the official ball thrower.

One day I noticed some red sores around Baron's mouth. After the veterinarian I worked for took a biopsy, Baron was diagnosed as having a mast-cell tumor, a particularly nasty cancer. Baron continued without any outer visible symptoms of disease. He had a great attitude and energy.

I waited to share the news with Ryan until be came

home to work for summer vacation. Ryan and Baron spent some wonderful time together that summer. August approached and the return of school loomed in the near future. Ryan and I started talking. Ryan said, "Mom, I can't go back to school knowing Baron's going to die. I have to be here for him."

We were scheduled to go to McCall, Idaho, the coming weekend to help build a dock. Baron loved the water and this was one of his favorite places. Ryan and his dad would pound a nail, drill a hole, put a screw into the dock, and throw the stick for Baron. When they were too busy to throw the stick, Baron would drop it in the water himself, run to the end of the dock, and take flight, launching himself into the water to retrieve.

That day Baron played his heart out swimming and retrieving for thirteen hours in a row. We finished the dock and came home to Sun Valley the next day. Baron developed a temperature of 105 degrees. I rushed him to the vet clinic where I worked. There they hooked him up to IVs, and tried to keep him cool. Ryan slept with him at the clinic that night and Baron passed away the next morning, two weeks before Ryan was supposed to return to school.

Ryan and his dad spent the afternoon together crying and building a beautiful wooden cross with Baron's name engraved on it. We knew that we had to take Baron's body back to McCall so he could be buried facing the lake he loved. We placed Baron in the back of the Explorer and headed for the lake. Two hundred miles later, we arrived. We decided upon a gravesite, dug the hole as we cried, and laid our beloved comedian to rest facing the water. Just as we finished, a beautiful iridescent black feather floated down and landed on his grave as if to say, "See, it's okay, my spirit is flying."

For a long time, whenever I would come home and walk up to the front door I could still hear Baron bark his welcome. I told my husband I could hear Baron whenever I walked up to the front door and he thought I was crazy until one day he also heard the Baron's welcoming bark.

I don't think we ever lose that essence of true love when it is given so unconditionally as it is by a pet. There are no strings attached to that love, it is pure, and it adds to that love quotient in our lives that determines the frequency at which we vibrate.

Ryan experienced great difficulty in letting go of his beloved companion, and one night Baron came to him in a dream and said, "If you remember me in sorrow, don't remember me at all."

There is a quote by Sir Walter Scott that states, "I have sometimes thought of the final cause of dogs having such short lives, and I am quite satisfied it is in compassion to the human race, for if we suffer so much in losing a dog after an acquaintance of ten or twelve years, what would it be if they were to live double that time?"

Besides graduating from college Suma cum Laude,

Ryan had learned the lesson Baron came to teach him. Love grows in boundless ways when we take responsibility for it.

Angels in the Orchard
By Winston

Roberta and I had been living with her parents in Boise after our summer exodus from Texas. Shelly, Roberta's father, had a knee replacement, and we stayed the winter to help him deal with living in their split-level home with his new knee. His one-acre property had a large orchard and garden and I had helped him by doing things his new knee joint would not let him do, such as pruning and running the rototiller. That spring the orchard was gloriously alive with a riot of blooms. It looked like there would be a grand crop of apples, pears, cherries, plums, and peaches. The four apricot trees were absolutely laden with blossoms.

In my estimation there is nothing to compare with a tree-ripened apricot, and I was looking forward to the summer, when I would get to sample and pick the crop. Shelly told me that his trees had never produced any apricots since he had planted them seven or eight years before because the orchard was in a cold spot and even a light freeze seemed to hang heavy there. Apricots are highly susceptible because they bloom early.

Bad news. A hard freeze was coming to the Boise valley and the expected 28-degree temperature would wipe out most of Shelly's orchard. He had no smudge pots or windmills like the commercial orchards did. There was nothing that we could do.

I had been reading about the Findhorn garden in Scotland, which relied on a certain amount of angelic participation in growing successful gardens and orchards farther north than anyone else. I decided to conduct a limited experiment with the apricot trees to see if there was any truth to what I had read. I went to the apricot trees and specifically asked for warmth and protection. I visualized in my imagination an angel sitting in each apricot tree spreading protection and warmth for this particular frost and any others yet to come that season. I also visualized the trees laden with sweet luscious fruit for the summer harvest. I imagined how much I was going to enjoy picking and eating those perfect specimens. I spent about thirty minutes meditating, imagining, and visualizing in great detail all aspects of the protection and appreciation for those apricots.

The hard freeze came. The next morning we looked at the devastation of the orchard. All the trees except the apricots showed varying degrees of frost damage. Blossoms covered the ground or hung limp from the trees. The four apricot trees, however, were perfect. That summer they produced bountifully for the first time. The fruit was fantastic. We gorged ourselves on tree-ripened apricots. We made jam. We gave fruit to friends and family. We canned apricots.

I have since conducted similar experiments and I know that working with nature rather than trying to eradicate all the pests and weeds is a viable solution to gardening woes. Petitioning for higher protection also works. I want to have my own place again and teach little Spencer about gardens, angels and visualizing outcomes.

Bubba
By Dolora

Shortly after my daughter's move to Missoula, Montana, she experienced an overwhelming need for a dog, specifically a chocolate Labrador. It was not practical for her to get a puppy, as she was in class a great deal of the day, so Wendy decided that an adult Lab would suit her perfectly.

When Wendy gets clear on what she wants, she pursues it with a vengeance until the desire manifests itself into reality.

Wendy first checked in with the humane society in Missoula in her search for the perfect companion. No luck. She went to the grocery store for food and a young man wearing an apron started talking to her about a chocolate Lab that needed a home. The man had a name tag on his apron and Wendy noticed that his name was Alvin. She inquired about the age and sex of the dog and was informed that "Bubba" was a six-year-old male chocolate Lab.

She drove out right away to meet the dog. He was very depressed, not at all clean, and he was very thin. The owners wanted $100 for him. His cage hadn't been cleaned for months. It seemed he had been trained as a hunting dog, but after Bubba's owner got married, the wife didn't bond with the Lab and as a result he was dispatched to the back forty acres and then neglected.

Wendy was appalled, and refused to pay for the dog. She told the caretakers she would just take the dog for them and they agreed. Bubba was so depressed all he could do was pace and cry. Wendy had a veterinarian go over him, updated his vaccinations, had him neutered, gave him a bath and took him to obedience classes.

Bubba just had no clue what was going on and he stuck to Wendy like a tick sticks to a sheep even though he was anxious and a bit skittish even around her. He refused to retrieve and he was always enormously hungry. When no one was watching, Bubba would climb up on the counters and devour any food in sight.

Wendy had had Bubba about three weeks when I decided to go visit her. I took toys for him, one being a stuffed chicken that crowed. Bubba sort of liked this toy but still would not "go fetch." I was doing a workshop over in Hamilton, Montana, with a group of twenty ladies, and Wendy had decided to join us. We were all out in the forest gathered around a group of trees. Not far from us, Bubba was in the car with the windows open. This seminar was of the spiritual nature and we had started toning when I decided that it would be a good idea to do an exercise to call in the angels. We started -EE Nu Ra when all of a sudden Bubba jumped out of the car, walked into the middle of the circle of women and sat down. He just stayed there absorbing all the energy. We were a little surprised, but no one ob- jected. That evening when we took Bubba home he started playing for the first time.

Bubba was finally moving into a state of trust with Wendy. He kept his eye on her, never letting her out of his sight. Bubba's life-style changed. He started going to college classes with Wendy, lying under her desk or workspace. The instructors allowed his presence because he was so well behaved. He and Wendy both graduated from the University of Montana. Often times the dean would refer to Bubba as the brightest student in the class.

Wendy went back to the grocery store to thank the young man who had given her the information about the dog. However, she was informed that they had never had an employee by the name of Alvin.

Bubba and Wendy moved home to Sun Valley after graduation. Bubba's insecurity about food still remained, but he was improving.

Miracles can always happen if you make mental and emotional space for them! Bubba lived with me off and on for a period of about nine months. During that time he resolved his issues with food, and so I didn't have to make sure the counters were clear of morsels. However, after he moved to Virginia with Wendy, I discovered two bags of marshmallows with doggie teeth marks in them. He had removed them from the pantry and stored them in my sewing area, just in case life became uncertain and not sweet enough.

One day Bubba was out running in the woods in Virginia at the farm where Wendy lived. He took a flying leap into the air, and severed his spine, dying instantly. Wendy called me, sobs wracking her body, to give me the news. My heart filled with sorrow for her loss. Wendy was devastated without her companion. Within a week, though, a beautiful male chocolate Lab swam across the lake on the farm where she lived, walked into her office, and laid down on Bubba's bed. Reggo is still with her.

Bubba was truly Wendy's gift from the angels and she was his. It always amazes me that what we need is always provided for us, if we get out of the way and let it happen.

Findhorn/Perelandra Experiment
By Winston

Some of my fondest memories of my maternal grandfather, Elmer Lot Howard, are of him working in his
garden. He and Grandma lived in an apartment over our
garage for the last ten years of their lives. Grandpa had
always had a garden and Grandma always had flowers
and indoor plants. They both had green thumbs and the
things they grew looked pretty and tasted wonderful. I
didn't realize how much of a stamp Grandpa had made
on me until his death, when I cried for three days. So
much for my being a macho-man of twenty-five.

I had my first garden in Seattle in a vacant lot adja-
cent to the house we rented on Thirty-sixth Street. I
borrowed some books on gardening from the library.
The owner of the vacant lot was our landlord and he
gave me permission to plant a garden. I rented a rotor-
tiller, churned up the lot, raked the soil, sorted out the
rocks and weeds, and started to plant.

As a teenager, one of my jobs every spring and fall
had been to rototill the garden. I had never done much
else in Grandpa's garden because it was definitely his
domain, not mine. However, when I started planting I
found I had access to a lot of information about gardening apart from the books I was reading. All I had to do
was ask myself, "What would Grandpa do?" In my brain
I had a whole library of mental videos of Grandpa as he

gardened. Spacing, mounding potatoes, talking to the plants, thinning, pruning tomatoes, staking beans, all these procedures and more were in my head. I took the library books back. It was much more fun to "watch the videos," especially because it made me feel close to Grandpa again. Needless to say, my first garden flourished.

Since that first garden, I have always had an interest in gardening even though my lifestyle has not often allowed me to pursue it to the degree I would like. When we first moved to the Trout Lake Valley, we rented a trailer house. We had poor soil, too much shade, and not much time to even consider gardening. I had read about the Findhorn community in Scotland and their many successes growing larger plants farther north than anyone had before. Then I read a book about a contemporary garden in Virginia, called *Perelandra Garden Workbook—A complete guide to gardening with nature intelligences*, by Machaelle Small Wright. I was fascinated by the system of asking nature, Devas, and the plants themselves about plant locations, partnering, and energy enhancement. It was not so far away from me asking my dead grandfather, "What would you do?"

It was late August and my available soil was poor and shaded. What an opportunity to really test some of these new principles. I needed some good natural fertilizer to revitalize my poor soil. A friend up the road raised llamas, so I cleaned his sheds and drove home with several pickup loads of free composted llama manure. I borrowed a tiller and churned up a patch of earth about twenty-feet square, and worked in the llama dung. I knew I was stacking the deck against myself as I planted a garden just before Labor Day, but I used some of the Perelandra techniques and we ended up eating greens, turnips, carrots, and Brussels sprouts well into November.

My grandfather was not a religious person, and he did not go to church. He taught me by example that what you love — be it animals, plants, or people — will respond in like fashion. As he walked through his garden I watched him unconsciously reach out to "pet" the plants and trees. I didn't understand until I found myself doing it, too. He used to tell my mother to, "Wipe your feet off before you go into the garden!" His little joke revealed the reverence he bestowed on his garden. Talking to a plant, asking it where it would like to grow, when and how much to be watered, or asking for help from the governing entities that control living things, all demonstrate love and respect, which causes a similar response.

I know a family in the Trout Lake Valley who have a dairy farm that has been in existence since the 1890s, when their ancestors settled there. Whether or not they know of Findhorn or Perelandra, they have been practicing most of the principles for at least five generations. The reverence they have for their land and animals is readily apparent to anyone who drives by. They use modern machinery, organic from-the-cow fertilizer, and few if any pesticides, herbicides, or hormonal injections. They made the transition from a regular to an "organic" dairy a few years ago and were able to obtain a higher price for their milk. Without especially intending to, they had already been meeting most of the more stringent requirements to qualify through their long-standing family practice.

Monty, Orin, or someone from the family "tucks the cows in" every night before going to bed. "Tucking the cows in," I am sure, includes both the visual check to see that all is in order and prayers for the continued well-being of and gratitude for the blessings the cows continue to give to the family. They plant a garden every year in a somewhat shaded area for their own use. One look at it is enough to see and feel the reverence they hold for the living things in their charge. I was privileged to have five of their children in my classes at Trout Lake School.

Since God is the source of love, he honors all our attempts at loving a tomato, kitten or child. It is the most important lesson I can pass on to my little son, Spencer.

The Crying Tree
By Dolora

There is a tree outside Sun Valley, Idaho, whose size is such that it takes four large adults or six children with their arms outstretched to complete a circle around it. Rumor has it that this tree could not be climbed or cut, and that it wept. Needless to say, I was fascinated by the story and I endeavored to find someone who could lead me to this magical tree. My search was successful.

One fall Saturday afternoon my husband and my son and I set out on our journey to see this mystical creation. We hiked up an old abandoned logging road and came to a very large fir tree with pitch dripping down its whole being; indeed giving it the appearance of weeping. I marveled at the size of the giant. My husband and son were eager to continue their hike. I reluctantly left and I thanked the tree for its presence on the planet. At this time the tree telepathed the message that it wanted to talk to me. My first instinct was, "Yeah, right," I'm going to talk to a tree," but my curiosity was piqued and I sent the tree the message that I would return alone. It took me a month to return.

I gently placed my hands on the tree and this is the story the tree telepathed to me. It took twenty minutes for this story to be dictated.

"It is I, the spirit of the Monarch tree. I am truly glad to have this opportunity to tell you my history. I was born long before the beginning of time. I come from a long line of master trees whose duty it was to forest the earth creating oxygen for all living things. I caused the green grasses to grow and the mighty waters to flow.

"In the beginning my power was very small, but my spirit was great and I kept the vision my ancestors gave me in my heart. My roots grew large and deep into this hillside so that I could stand until the end of time if I so chose to hold that vision. I have many children, some of them reaching to the far corners of this earth. I am perceived as both a male and female tree, and that is correct. I have the power within myself to give birth to as many trees as I feel that earth can nourish.

"My mission has been a sacred mission, as the earth has needed my efforts to grow and flourish. I grew strong and tall and my mission was easy. When my brothers the Indian humans came, they honored my life. The white man came and did not know his soul's connection with the trees of the forest, and he started a reaction against the forest people, not honoring them or asking their permission to be cut. Many of my precious children died for the white man thus creating great mourning among the trees. You will find many areas of the earth where the tree people refuse to grow because man does not acknowledge the gifts of the trees.

"I was several hundred years old when the white man came to remove me from this forest and I became so angry that I shook and shook, thus keeping my life as they could not cut me down. That was many years ago, but it made me realize my powers over the man-forces on earth.

"Many of my children still stand and we are starting to sing with joy. The wind carries our song as we see mankind starting to honor the standing people, the people who create so much so that man can live and breathe.

"One time I almost lost my life when the people of the sky were dancing. I was struck by one of the great bolts of father lighting and started to burn. The thunder people saw this and were dismayed that their dancing could cause me such pain. Immediately the cloud people poured rain over my whole body, putting out the fire and preserving my life. Let me tell you I have many wounds from that incident. The scar in my side was caused at that time. Much flesh was ripped from my body. My roots have had to grow very deep in order that I may stand on this hillside.

"I honor mother earth with my children and my spirit to continue to live. I shed my tears for the lack of knowledge mankind has concerning the purpose of all tree people, but soon I will cry no more as man is starting to understand that he cannot live without the trees. Thank you for listening to my story. In the name of all creation and creative beings, I remain one with you."

The Monarch Tree

The tree died within a year of telling me this story, but every year I journey to its place and marvel at its majesty, even in death.

The Dove
By Dolora

In 1996, about June, I was having a dilemma concerning the work I was doing. I had been offered three different positions in which to work. I had not been seeking a change at this time so I wondered about these unsolicited opportunities and if the universe was trying to tell me something. All the positions paid approximately the same dollar amount. Benefits were varied and each position had an appeal of its own. I couldn't seem to come to an intelligent decision about which situation was best for me — the one I was currently in at the veterinary clinic, or one of the other two employment opportunities.

I asked the universe for a sign. I picked the sign of a dove. A dove represents peace and tranquility in my mind. It was also the symbol for land in the story of Noah's ark, and doves are known as messengers of God.

My criteria then became, wherever I would first see or hear about a dove, that conversation would be the sign that I belonged in that place. It would be the position that would bring my soul its greatest growth and happiness. My intent was to go to each business and see what happened.

I felt comfortable with my decision. I was no longer stewing about what to do and I believed I had a foolproof method for figuring out God's will for me or my divine will for myself. It doesn't matter what you source as your highest good, as long as you acknowledge that there truly is a source higher than confusion and ego.

The next morning I got up as usual 5:30 AM, made lunches, fixed breakfast, took care of the dog, showered, dressed and drove the sixteen miles to work. I made the rounds of the animal hospital cages checking to see if any changes had occurred during the night. In one of the top small cages in the treatment room there was a very lovely bird. People often brought wild birds into the clinic, especially in the summers — owls, eagles, hawks, robins, sparrows, and falcons, all with a variety of problems. I didn't have a clue as to what kind of bird it was, so I asked Mark, my boss and the owner of the clinic, what kind of a bird it was. He replied. "D, that is a dove." He said it was the first dove that he had ever treated in fifteen years of business.

Well, I was astounded at this quick response to the sign I had asked for. My ego started telling me it was just coincidence. My higher guidance said, "You ask for a sign, and we give you a sign, and yet you are still in doubt."

The phone started ringing and I went up to the front desk to answer it. I don't remember the person's name; however, they asked me to check their dog's vaccination history. I turned on the computer, typed in the client's name, and asked them for their dog's name. They answered, "Dove." Needless to say I mentally thanked my own higher source for the sign. I had again been given the sign my ego had asked for. Such validation!

About a week later I had the courage to share this incident with my boss. I was holding a dog as he was working on it and I was explaining my dilemma to him. I informed him of the other job offers and how I had asked for a sign as to which one to take.

My boss said, "I wished I had known that all you needed was a dove to make you stay. I would have gotten you a whole box of doves."

I continued to work at the veterinary clinic. We built a new state-of-the-art facility with a courtyard filled with vibrant blooming flowers during spring and summer. Waterfalls and fishponds add to the peaceful environment. My boss gives me a great deal of credit for helping build the business to this point. I have received much growth in this situation, learning to deal with the emotions of the twenty-two people with whom I work.

I look back and I realize how my job has pushed forward my awareness of compassion. I have had to step back and become aware of how my actions affect others. I have had to learn that not everybody perceives things as I do, and that their perception is equally as valid as mine is. Being manager of the facility requires a great deal of energy. Dealing with egos is difficult; doing it lovingly requires even greater skill. Learning to deal with my own ego in a loving way has been the most difficult.

I often wonder if I am truly equipped to handle the

job. So once again I considered asking the universe for a sign. Was it time to leave the position? I vacillated between asking again for the sign of a dove, or if another sign was appropriate.

A friend of mine gave me a work of art by Brian Andreas with wonderfully colorful characters on it. This is the story and the author states it is mostly true. The print has some words that read,

I used to wait for a sign, she said, before I did anything. Then one night I had a dream & an angel in black tights came to me & said, You can start any time now, and then I said, Is this a sign?" & the angel started laughing & I woke up. Now, I think the whole world is filled with signs, but if there's no laughter, I know they're not for me.

I love laughter, maybe that will be my next sign. Wherever abundant laughter occurs, that is where I belong.

A Rock with a Hole In It

By Dolora

Again I nestle in my chair with my blanket and my favorite pen. Do you know how important having the perfect writing implement is when you are creating a story? Some people use a computer, another author I've met writes in the bathtub. Me, I cherish the silence of the wee small hours of the morning when my house has no sounds except the gurgling of the water fountain sitting on the table to my left. This is a very special water fountain because I made it myself with the rock I found on the top of Grand Targhee ski area a few years ago.

Maybe you want to know why a rock would be so special because it came from the top of a small ski area in Eastern Idaho on the west face of the Grand Teton. It was June in 1997 and my husband had asked me to go with him to a Western Regional Ski Conference to market his employer's technological expertise. It was a small group of people exchanging knowledge on the top of the mountain. The weather was very wet and I had spent the greater part of two days enjoying being curled up with a good book. I love to read, especially spiritual books about miraculous events. Even small events fill me with the joy of the possibility of having magical moments in my life.

The weather had cleared and Grand Targhee was opening the chairlift, so the conference participants

could have an easy trip to the top of the mountain. I
had decided that I wanted to find a rock, a powerful
rock. According to Native American tradition, a rock
with a hole in it has power. The hole represents the
womb of woman and is a great source of creativity and
strength. The ride up the chairlift was cold and windy. I
stepped off the chairlift grateful for my jacket. A million
rocks covered the landscape, mostly shale in some form.
I started walking, head down, thinking about finding
that perfect stone. Within five minutes I found a rock
about four inches across at its broadest point. In the
center of this heart-shaped rock is a hole about one half
to three-quarters of an inch in diameter. I was amazed
and pleased by my instant good fortune. Not only did
the rock have a hole, but it is also was heart-shaped.
What a bonus. I put it in the pocket of my rain jacket
and headed for the chairlift. The wind was intense and I
was anxious to get down the mountain and into a more
gentle location.

My husband and I and several other conference
participants all retired to a small bar to socialize and have
a beer. I pulled out my rock and shared my find with
everyone at the table. Someone in the group noticed
that a wonderful fossil of a sea creature was embedded in
its side.

I ask myself, What is the probability of finding a
rock, heart-shaped, with a hole at the center with a sea
fossil embedded in its side, on the top of a mountain in

Eastern Idaho in a matter of five minutes? I decided that the chances of all that taking place were pretty miraculous. Ah, another small miracle, I love it.

What is the lesson here? I was very clear on my intent. I had no emotional attachment to the outcome, and the manifestation was almost instantaneous. I think this is the key to creating what you want. Be totally clear on your desire and then release any emotional need to manifest it. Allow joy. When doubt doesn't exist in your mind, the universe loves to support your desires.

Walking With Donner
By Dolora

I sit in my favorite overstuffed chair, which is soft and
flows around my body. There is room to bring my legs
into that comfortable position — crossed as if sitting on
the ground in Indian fashion, yet my back is supported.
The blanket I cover myself with is tattooed with little
bits of dog hair from my beloved St. Bernard "Donner."
This dog so reads my soul. He pushes me outside as
often as possible and causes me to walk at a leisurely
pace, a pace that allows him to be a botanist. A pace that
allows him to catalog every scent, every change that has
taken place since yesterday.

Donner is my dog although originally we thought he
would be my husband's dog. However, both Donner
and I resist the driving force and discipline that seems to
make my husbands life work. My husband likes to
charge up the hills behind our house, timing himself
with his stopwatch to see if he is more fit than the last
time he made the climb. He receives pleasure from
knowing that he has improved his time.

Donner and I amble. He is on his leash, but the
word "heel" is foreign to him as he meanders from side
to side, eventually finding his way into the creek to drink
as much as he needs to drink when the sun is shining on
his back and it is warm outside.

Donner drinks and drools a bit, then he slowly lowers

himself belly deep into the pond the beaver dam has created. He lounges in the pool for a while and then slowly pulls himself up the bank, shakes out his beautiful fur, and we continue on our walk.

His favorite occupation is making friends on the bike path. Donner is impossible to ignore and he has never met a stranger. Wiggling all over, he will sniff them in all the important places in order to get acquainted. Donner is like a magnet that draws people to us as we walk. How my social life has increased from walking this large, hairy beast. People call to determine what our walking schedule is so that they can participate.

Often times on walks with old friends or new ones, the conversations turn to the spiritual nature of things, or how energy works, for this is my passion. Very rarely do we engage in small talk because politics and gossip do not fill my soul. Seeing people move into a state of greater joy and greater connectedness fills my being. When I walk with Donner, unconditional love starts to happen. We feel the sun almost every day in Sun Valley, Idaho. Rarely during the day do you move in grayness. Rivers and mountains provide a beauty that ups your vibration. It is impossible to be here and not shift your energy when you are outside.

Donner and I walk about three miles every day. Sometimes I resist and even resent Donner's persistence, but he loves his schedule. Every morning, Donner comes to my side of the bed, puts his massive head by

my knee and starts breathing heavily. He is impossible to
ignore as he seems to say, "It's time to get up! Another
day has arrived." He informs you that he truly needs his
hind haunches massaged and his tummy rubbed. Going
out to the bathroom is not important, but he has experienced as many hours as he could survive without being
loved. His limit seems to be about eight hours without
receiving physical affection. I marvel at his honesty and
knowingness. Wouldn't we as humans be so much better
off if we acknowledged our need for touching, holding,
and affection?

What if we knew our needs and demanded that they
be met with the honesty of a dog? As soon as Donner
has had his love, he walks into the bathroom and hangs
his head over the tub. He expects you to turn on the
faucet and give him a fresh drink of water. He hates
water just in a bowl. You had better be sure that the
water is cold because hot water is not his thing, and if a
Saint Bernard has ever frowned at you, you know you
have really screwed up.

Donner is a living example of so many things in my
life that work. He knows how to be relaxed. Very little
bothers him except the wind when it gusts hard and roars
around the corners of the house. Donner likes his world
peaceful, and juicy. He loves the water, the snow (which
he eats in mouthfuls), and being outside. He adores
being touched and loves sharing the big chair with Mom.
He cherishes quiet time after eating and he snores with

contentment about twenty hours of the day, only waking up and interrupting your project when he needs love.

Donner is a constant reminder of unconditional love in my life. He also reminds me that I need to allow myself time to observe nature and all the spectacular wildlife in this valley. Donner's very being telegraphs this message, "See, it takes just the necessities of life to be joyful. Simplicity can fill your soul."

Donner is a constant reminder of the simple magic of life, for every path is a new exploration for him. He's never bored even if he has walked this path countless times before. He always finds joy.

Donner is truly an inspirational and angelic presence in my life. Dog is God spelled backwards and is a reflection of that unlimited life force within called God.

Perfect Timing

In each of the following instances I was given the opportunity and awareness that I was being provided with a path that would bring joy and create flow in my life or that of others. All things work together for the greater good if we but listen to that inner voice. Dolora

The timeliness of multiple events seems to suggest something beyond coincidence. If what you need is supplied precisely when you need it, that can make a case for being constantly monitored. It gives a feeling of peace and makes you feel secure. Winston

One-Lane Bridge
By Winston

I was headed back to college in a raging snowstorm in
the winter of 1961. I had come home to get my term
paper in scientific terminology typed. Mom typed the
paper for me and I was going back to the University of
Idaho at Moscow. The road was slick and it was snowing
hard. With this weather and the icy roads I averaged
about thirty-five miles an hour. Going from Bonners
Ferry to Moscow on Highway 95 would take five or six
hours.

The old stretch of Highway 95 between Bonners
Ferry and Naples followed Deep Creek, crossing the
creek several times via some narrow, concrete bridges.
The bridges had been recently reclassified and posted as
one-lane. We had been driving across them for years and
passing another car was not too scary, passing a truck was
exciting, two trucks passing was a game of chicken on
who would brake first. I was approaching one of the last
bridges before Naples, which had a downhill grade to the
bridge on both sides. As I came over the top of the hill I
saw a gasoline truck and trailer at the same point on the
other side, coming toward me. Both of us were going to
arrive at the bridge at the same time. Going across that
bridge with a gasoline truck under those road conditions
could end in a fiery disaster.

I tapped the brakes ever so lightly, and started fishtailing from side to side although my forward speed stayed the same. I couldn't imagine that it would be possible to cross the ice- and snow-covered bridge with the truck and its drifting trailer, which was oscillating back and forth across the center line. I decided to ditch the car in the snow bank and avoid the bridge altogether. I turned the wheel and moved toward the snow bank, but it was frozen, so I just bounced back into the center of the road. However, now my car was positioned broadside to the oncoming truck.

At that point, time shifted into slow motion, and my thinking became incredibly clear. I was totally calm and I made a number of perfect moves. First I managed to straighten the car by correcting for the broadside skid. I could see that the trailer of the truck was still oscillating two or three feet across the center line, but there was nothing I could do except keep steering in a straight line. I made a number of micro adjustments before reaching the bridge. The duals of the trailer were in my lane, but in my peripheral vision I saw a big puff of diesel exhaust as the truck driver accelerated. That acceleration pulled the rear wheels of the trailer back into his lane at the very last moment. I saw the driver's face as we passed each other; he looked as scared as I felt.

I found the next turn-out and pulled off the road. My body shook for twenty or thirty minutes before I ventured back on the road. It was a slow trip back to school and I got a C on the term paper.

This memory has stayed fresh even though it happened years ago. I would like to talk to the man in the gasoline truck. We both did some inspired driving that night. He and I seemed in perfect control while it happened. Trying to ditch the car was my last Winston move. When the time shift to slow motion happened, all moves became automatic and perfect. There were many small corrections to accelerator, brake, and steering. I was in control, yet detached, observing all as it happened.

And yet, what was amazing is that the control seemed to come from outside of myself. I have had enough of these experiences to know now that there are available sources of help and guidance beyond our imagining. I don't remember asking specifically for help. I do remember wondering with passion, "What do I do now?" Something outside of my normal self took charge. I became a detached observer. This memory has remained strong and I have occasional flashbacks. I never have been as good a driver as I was on that bridge. I am pretty sure the driver of the gasoline truck and trailer felt the same way.

I asked, "What do I do now?" in complete desperation after all else I had tried failed, my prayer was immediately answered.

Connecting with a Mentor
By Winston

I met Mr. Lockery the summer of 1959, just after I had finished my junior year in high school. The University of Idaho organized an annual summer music camp where young musicians came to play their instruments, sing in the choir, and study one-on-one with a university instructor. I had been to the music camp the year before, but did not take any private lessons. Private lessons cost extra and I wasn't brave enough to think about playing or singing one-on-one for anyone that first year. My voice had changed during my freshman year from soprano to one-octave-baritone. As soon as that happened I started singing in the Methodist church choir directed by my mother. Everyone in her family sang and it was expected that I would sing, too. I could read music and I received a lot of positive re-enforcement about my singing from my immediate family.

When the University of Idaho traveling choir, the Vandaleers, directed by Glen Lockery performed that spring in our town, two of the Vandaleers stayed at our house. I was very impressed with their performance and I decided to take some voice lessons that summer with Glen Lockery. I thought it might be possible for me to sing in the Vandaleers when I went to college in another year.

I don't remember much about my first voice lessons.

The short time at music camp was not time enough to do much more than start to produce a basic sound. I liked studying with Mr. Lockery; he was kind and I felt I learned from him. At our last lesson he asked me to come back to Moscow to sing at a conference in August. I gave it no more thought until he called me a few months later. It turned out that I was to be the adolescent voice for a demonstration lesson in front of members of the National Association for the Teachers of Singing. I sang my song and the adjudicator worked with me in front of all those teachers. Anyone who has taught voice for a while knows the limitations of a late-blooming baritone of seventeen.

In the fall of 1960, I enrolled at the University of Idaho as a pre-med major. I had taken all the math and science courses offered at our high school, although I received only B's and C's. There was family pressure on me to do something at which I could make a decent living even though in high school I had excelled in music and drama. I talked to Mr. Lockery that fall about joining the choir, but my chemistry and zoology labs met at the same time the choir rehearsed. He told me to keep in touch. I started playing in the university band in my second semester because it met an hour later and only three times a week.

I survived the first year, but my grades were not good enough to send me to medical school. During the second year my courses got tougher. Quantitative and

Qualitative Analysis, and Comparative Anatomy were major courses in my curriculum. By Christmas I knew I was in trouble. I received notice from the Dean's office that I had one more semester to raise my grades or be expelled from school for scholastic reasons.

Mr. Lockery called me and asked me how I was doing. I told him that I was in trouble scholastically, although I suspected that somehow he already knew. He invited me to come see him, and during our meeting he asked me why I was in pre-med. I told him that it was a choice that pleased my parents. When he asked me what I would choose to do for myself, I was able to answer him easily. I loved singing and playing instruments. I couldn't officially change majors until the following fall, but I could start taking voice lessons second semester. He called my pre-med advisor and indicated that I would be changing majors as soon as possible.

I wrote my parents and told them I would be changing majors because I needed to be doing something I loved rather than something that would make a good living. They accepted my choice and gave me their support.

I looked forward to those voice lessons every week and always came prepared. I spent hours in the practice hall. Working on my voice lessons gave me hope. The A's I received from voice lessons and band raised my grade point enough to keep me in school until I became

a freshman in music the fall semester of my junior year.
Then Mr. Lockery asked me to sing with the touring
choir on their spring tour. I learned and memorized all
the music by my first rehearsal.

I don't know what went on between Mr. Lockery and
my pre-med advisor that spring semester, but somehow I
stayed in school. My self-esteem, grades, and success in a
career all started from Mr. Lockery's interest, and guidance. His actions were the life preserver that saved my
drowning college career. I wonder about how different
my life would be had he not entered it when he did. I
wonder at the timing of his phone call when I was in
despair.

I have been blessed with many mentors. I lived in
what my students think of as an unbelievable idyllic
family setting: two parents, mom in the home, grandparents in an apartment over the garage, two pairs of aunts
and uncles with cousins living only a short walk away. I
had the secure feeling that whatever happened I was
loved by a number of people. Besides family and Mr.
Lockery, there have been a number of other people who
have served as my mentors. Walt Snodgrass, Mary
Curtis-Verna, Jess Walters, Lee Unger, and many others
all appeared in my life to give me direction, help, or love
when I needed it. Mr. Lockery was the most dramatic
example of a mentor because he intervened when I was
in my darkest despair.

I love all those people who seem to have been arranged and scheduled in my life. There seems to have been a grand design to let me live my life in a way that far exceeds my craft and abilities.

V. D.

By Dolora

In the world of medical technology V.D. is short for venereal disease. However, in this story it refers to Vernon Douglas Folz, my immunology professor at Kansas State University. V.D. was also my advisor. He made sure that my last semester in college was all in order. There was only one way my schedule could work in order for me to get the classes I needed to graduate. My husband was in the military and we would be leaving the area at the end of the term. Tiny, as Dr. Folz was also called, pulled all the computer cards ahead of schedule so that I would be sure and have the necessary classes.

Tiny taught the course in which we learned about antigens and antibodies, blood typing, and cross-matching, and naturally he taught us how to test for V.D. He was an excellent instructor with a sense of humor and good organizational skills. Whenever there was a long incubation period in the laboratory section of the course, he would tell us to go to the student union and get a cup of coffee. We just needed to be back in time to read the results of the tests we were performing. As students in immunopathology, we spent 20 hours a week in Tiny's class.

I finished up my course work at Kansas State and then proceeded to Boise to complete a year-long internship at St. Luke's Hospital. I was amazed at how well prepared I was to continue my education. Dr. Folz had made sure we were ready for the next step. I was so well prepared that I wound up teaching some of the graduate technicians the information Tiny had given us. The pathologists on staff even remarked about the quality of information I had.

There was a little voice inside of me that kept prompting me to write to Dr. Folz and tell him what a good job he had done as a teacher. I continually put off doing this but the message would not go away. Finally, one day I just sat down and wrote the letter and mailed it off to Dr. Folz in care of the College of Arts and Sciences, Kansas State University.

About two months after I wrote the letter an envelope arrived in the mail from the Dean, College of Arts and Sciences, KSU. The gist of the letter was this. Dr. Folz had brought the letter to the dean, beaming with pride in his accomplishment. He'd told the dean that his life had truly been validated. Dr. Folz died from cancer within two months of receiving the letter.
Ask me now if I am glad I listened to that still small voice. There is never any deed so insignificant that it cannot change someone's life. Any time you hear that voice, take the time to follow through. Be vulnerable, express your love whenever possible, it may be the thing that gives meaning to someone's journey. God bless you, Tiny, you made my life easier because you insisted I learn

the basics upside down and backwards.

That still small voice inside is often the prompting of your guardian angel, giving you messages that make the world a better place to live. Get quiet inside everyday and you can hear the voice of God telling you how to love the people he brings into your path. Never question the opportunity to make someone feel good, never worry if they have difficulty receiving the gift. Give the gift anyway because it may be the very thing that changes their life forever.

The Warm Letter
By Winston

It was Saint Patrick's Day. My wife and I were expecting a baby. I was working on the marina in Tacoma and the crew was going to knock off early and go to one of the local bars where I was probably going to sing several Irish tunes. My wife phoned me at work just after lunch and said she had called the doctor about lack of movement by our baby, which was due any day. He asked her to come in for a sound scan immediately. My plan to hoist a few beers and sing some Irish tunes changed; I needed to be with my wife. I packed up my tools and drove the fifty miles I commuted twice a day with a sense of dread. The sound scan found no fetal heartbeats; our baby was dead.

If we wanted to try to have another baby the best opportunity would be for Roberta to deliver the baby naturally. They asked us to come in the following Monday and be induced when the full staff would be present. We spent the weekend crying and calling close friends and family. We had been married for almost eleven years and had been trying for a baby for about five years. The following Monday Roberta and I went to the maternity ward where she was hooked up to an IV, which would deliver the drug petosin until the baby was delivered naturally. All around us were the sights and sounds of pregnant mothers giving birth to live babies. It took three days because the baby was unable to respond to contractions like a live baby.

When we finished the process we were completely drained. We both wanted to see the baby, even though the staff recommended against it. Both of us thought our little girl, to be named Gretchen, was beautiful. We didn't have a funeral service or acknowledge the life we never met. We tried to pick up our lives and continue. Roberta took the next six weeks off as pregnancy leave and swam every day to regain her pre-pregnant body. I worked at the marina and sang at my church job every week although I couldn't sing solos. Somehow, performing would bring up the grief of losing our baby and I would cry, unable to sing.

I had been to Germany the previous fall to audition for German opera companies to try to get a contract so that Roberta and I and the baby could move to Germany and be supported by a continuing singing contract complete with medical benefits. I would be working as a full-time singer. The year before there had been over ten openings for lyric baritones; the year I went, there were two. My agent said he thought he could find a situation for me if I could stay longer than the month I had allotted myself. But if I stayed I would have to pay a lot more to extend my ticket, Roberta was pregnant at home alone, and I was running out of money.

I came back home and threw myself into working

eight or nine hours a day at the marina in Tacoma, commuting the fifty miles from Mountlake Terrace, and landscaping and finishing the house we had bought a year earlier. After the singing situation fell through, I decided to support our growing family by seeking a public school teaching contract in the spring. With the housing market booming we could sell our house and move out of Seattle to a place more like the quiet, wooded, mountainous, places where we had each grown up in Idaho. After the death of the baby it still seemed the best plan. I needed a change from singing, a change from the city, time to just work in my field and get my head straight.

I had been a successful teacher right out of school ten years earlier, had since achieved a master's degree, and had been singing professionally in Seattle for ten years. I knew I could get a job teaching music, hopefully some-place remote and beautiful. I activated and updated my placement file at the University of Washington, and screened places that we thought would fit our needs. I wrote letters, filled out applications, and waited for a response to interview.

One day late in April I came home from work about six PM, and as I grabbed the mail on my way into the house I noticed that one of the letters was uncommonly warm. When I looked at the return address from the warm letter I saw that it was from the school district in Polson, Montana, and I was flooded with the feeling that here is where we would be offered a job. I walked into the house and said to Roberta, "Here is where we are going." We went to Polson, interviewed, and I was offered the job, which we accepted. We moved the following fall.

I have never been able to logically explain why one letter in the middle of a stack of mail sitting in the mailbox for several hours should be warmer than the rest. It was a relief to know that our prayers had been answered. A change of scene and the challenge of new jobs would help us to heal. I was grateful for the personal message of the warm letter; it allowed me to approach the interview with confidence.

The House that Blew Down
By Winston

While we lived in Texas during the early eighties I worked as a carpenter framing houses when I wasn't performing. I had worked as a carpenter before in Seattle. Although I never made great money, I enjoyed working outside and it kept me in great physical condition. I worked for the same guys, off and on as I was available for a number of years both in Seattle and Texas. According to my bosses, there was always a spot for me even though I wasn't the most skilled or knowledgeable worker. I was always dependable, I showed up every day on time, sober and straight. I liked the work and it filled the gaps between singing gigs. The framing crew and my bosses occasionally came to my performances.

One day I went to Houston to audition for Mr. Lundquist in Steven Sondheim's, "A Little Night Music." Houston's Theater Under the Stars was producing a ten-year reunion performance and all the members of the cast, except the five-member Greek-style chorus, were either the original stars or nationally-known musical theater people. Hermoine Gingold, in her mid-eighties was wonderful recreating her original role. Julliet Prowse, movie actress and ballet dancer, who did the "Leggs" commercial, played the female lead opposite Larry Kert, the original Tony in "West Side Story."

The construction crew was working on two houses at

169

the same time. I was assigned to the three-story wood house and it was time to start putting rafters up, something I had more experience doing than the younger members of our crew. I would only be working Monday and Tuesday of the next week. Wednesday I would go to Houston to begin rehearsals. I had told my boss I wanted to work right up to the day I left to go to rehearsal. But on Friday, I decided I would rather spend the coming Monday and Tuesday studying my part, so Friday would be my last day until after I finished the show.

That weekend it rained a lot. Showers continued through Monday and Tuesday. I worked hard to get on top of my part and felt ready for the performance. Tuesday afternoon I was enjoying the luxury of having a beer and watching the local news when to my surprise my boss came on the television. A house had blown down. It was the house where I would have been working if I'd gone to work. A man was killed while setting rafters exactly where I would have been if I had been on the job. My Friday afternoon decision to take an extra two days off to study my part had saved me from being injured or killed.

A subsequent investigation determined that the house probably fell because of the combination of a unique set of circumstances: the exposed raw wood had absorbed a lot of rain over the weekend, and the twisting forces of the heavy wind gusts blowing up the draw caused the central bearing wall on the first floor to collapse, which brought the three-story structure down into a one-story pile. It was lucky that more of the guys weren't killed. I came home from Houston the next weekend for the funeral, and I visited with those who were still in the hospital.

My last-minute decision was not prompted by anything other than the predicted bad weather and a desire to spend some more time on getting secure in my part. I had no intuitive clue that something might happen. But I have had enough of these types of events in my life to know that it was another positive example of protection, rather than an episode of random chance, luck, or coincidence.

Angela
By Dolora

I didn't remember the date but Angela did — to the
moment — because it was an event that was life-changing for both of us. On October 5th, 1995, my friend
Deborra, along with several other people in Sun Valley,
were hosting a party for Conservation International.
This organization works all over the planet to save rain
forests, wildlife, wild rivers, and all of the natural, un-
spoiled places on the planet. They work at saving or
reclaiming as much life as possible. The organization is
based in Washington, D.C., with branches throughout
the world. People were here from all over the world,
about one hundred fifty of them.

Many celebrities were invited, including Adam West
and Harrison Ford. Harrison Ford was being honored as
the Man of the Year for Conservation International.
Since I believe that there are no coincidences, I knew
there was a reason my husband and I had been invited to
this function, but I had no idea what it was. I wandered
among the people circulating at the reception being held
at the Silver Creek sporting goods store in Ketchum. I
only knew about eight people in the gathering. Wine
was flowing freely; Harrison Ford told a funny story
about a wide-mouthed frog.

I remember searching the crowd asking, "Okay God,
why am I here? It can't possibly be for the social gather-

ing, or the one hundred dollars I could donate to the cause. There must be a bigger reason."

I noticed a beautiful, dark-haired woman in a pale blue vest and slacks, and I was drawn to her. Everywhere in the crowd I would turn, the lady in blue would be in my line of vision.

Finally I introduced myself, and told her how lovely she looked. I also said that I had no idea why I was at the party, but since her energy kept beckoning me, maybe it was important for us to know one another.

Angela Mast was her name and she was from Columbia, South America. She was married to an American working for Conservation International. She had no idea why she had decided to come to this particular event, but baby sitters and reservations just fell into place, allowing her to come along at the last minute.

The reception moved from Silver Creek to my friend Deb's house, where the dinner was being held. At Deb's house I showed Angela some wildlife pillows I had made for my friend. One had a bear appliquéd on it, and an owl graced the other pillow, with three-dimensional feathers crafted out of leather. Angela asked, "Do you know what the bear symbolizes according to Native American belief?"

"Yes," I answered. "Bear is about introspection, about knowing oneself. Bear is my totem. Whenever a bear crosses your path, you are supposed to go inside to seek your answer."

"How about owl?" Angela asked.

"Owl is Deb's totem," I replied. "Owl is about wisdom. It is called the night eagle. Owl is very heavy medicine when it crosses your path. It can indicate that you are to experience a death of some sort in your life, not necessarily death in the physical sense, but an ending to part of your current life."

Angela broke down and started sobbing. She told me that she lived in constant fear for herself and her family. She was terrified that her husband would be killed when he was in the jungles working on projects. She was constantly living in fear of losing those she loved. Angela cried, "Why am I here, why am I even alive?" I told her to look at her name. "Angela Mast." It would give her purpose, to be a beacon of angelic consciousness on the planet." I replied. Angela was shaking. We talked intently for the rest of the party, oblivious to anyone else in the room. Here we were, two seekers of spiritual truth, and we had been drawn together because each of us was looking for a deeper meaning in life, and in the social function we were attending.

Angela was staying in a hotel just up the road from my house. We decided to spend the following day together. I was going to take her and her friend to a natural hot springs about ten miles out of town. At ten AM the next morning we headed for the hot springs, four ladies on a spiritual quest. We meditated and toned, totally connecting ourselves with nature in every fiber of our being. I told Angela the story of meeting my guardian angel and how I no longer lived in fear. Angela was desperate to release her fear and move into empowerment. I gave Angela the same answers to her questions that my guardian angle had given me.

She asked, "What is God?"

I told her, "God is the life force within, nothing less, nothing more. It is the life force in everything, the trees, the rocks, the waters, all of life."

Angela asked, "Why are we here?"

I gave her the same answer I had been given. "Life is a gift, the purpose is joy."

Although I have probably spent only seventy-two hours in the company of Angela, we have communicated with each other monthly for the last seven years. Angela has changed from a person who walked in fear into a woman who walks in total love and peace. She constantly reaches out to others to help them past their fears, to help them become the truth of who they are.

If we each take time to touch just one person with our joy, with our peace, we can change the world. It starts within self. We move beyond fear and seek our own higher purpose.

No One Cares

By Dolora

My friend Angela had asked me to come to Washington, D.C., to see the crystals at the Smithsonian. Amazingly enough my husband happened to have a meeting in Baltimore that I was invited to attend. I checked things out and realized I could take a train from Baltimore to D.C. with no problem. I could hardly wait to see Angela. It had been four years since we had met. I wasn't even sure I would recognize her.

Angela called and said, "You have got to come because we have an important job to do." I wasn't really clear on what the job consisted of, but I love adventures and I wanted to go. I worked out the train schedule from Baltimore and grabbed the first early morning train to D. C. Cell phones in hand, we managed to find each other as Angela's voice guided me past unfamiliar landmarks to a fountain in front of the train station. Screaming with delight and tears running down our face, we jumped in her van and headed out.

As we approached the Smithsonian, the energy in the car was palpable. We were guided to a parking place immediately, which in itself was a small miracle. Angela and I really didn't know what we were doing other than we were being totally directed by an invisible force of which we were both conscious. The power we were feeling was beyond anything I had ever experienced.

Where was the energy coming from and what was its purpose? As we approached the Smithsonian buildings we passed a man, dressed neatly, but asking for money. As we walked by he was crying, "No one in the city cares! All I want to do is go home."

Angela stopped me and asked, "What did he say?"

"I'm not sure," I replied.

We decided to walk back and question him about his problem. He angrily told us," I parked incorrectly and they impounded my car. I only had two hundred dollars and I need two hundred and thirty-two dollars to get my car. I just want to get my family out of this city and go home to Philadelphia."

There was a bigger picture to this story. All this man wanted to do was go home - isn't that what we all want? Angela and I looked at each other and handed him the thirty dollars he still needed to get home. Not because we necessarily believed him, but because what he was asking was very symbolic to us.

We all want to go home to that spiritual place where we connect with God. This man was from the city of brotherly love. How could we not help? The request was truly in tune with the work Angela and I were attempting. We wanted to help all of mankind to go home. This stranger was amazed that we helped him. He asked. "What do you want me to do in return for the money?"

I told him, "Teach your children to cherish the planet,

to not destroy the earth's resources." We asked him to recycle whenever he could and to become a good steward of the planet on which he lived.

He asked, "Is that all?" He said he would comply with our request.

We entered the Smithsonian and the crystals were magnificent. I know that crystals can amplify and transmit energy. The size and the clarity of these crystals exceeded anything I had ever experienced. The energy around us was thick. You could feel the force with your hands although it was unseen. As Angela and I moved through the exhibit, we started a mantra that stated no longer do we as a people have to learn about the value of peace by living with war. We could now learn and teach our children about peace by living in peace. No longer would we learn the value of love by experiencing the opposite, hate. But rather we would learn love from experiencing love. We would now co-create light by being the radiance of our being. Love by being loving to everyone and everything that enters our field. We would experience truth by being the pieces of God that we are. Joy would be felt by rejoicing just because we are Light, Love, Truth, Joy, and Peace; these were the aspects of ourselves that we called into being here on Earth. These aspects would become the cornerstones of our new dimension. These are the pillars of our newly updated home. This is the message that we asked the crystals to amplify to the universe.

Angela and I toured all of the crystals and we declared freedom from duality with a prayer asking that the world might live in truth, peace, love, light, and joy. We were exhausted when we finished. Angela took me back to the train station and proceeded to drive home. She said she arrived home safely but had no consciousness of the trip. Something very special took place that day. The invisible energies with us were very powerful and tangible. Maybe the whole purpose was symbolic. As we move into the New Age, this Age of Aquarius, the time of taking care of your brother, we have to change our way of thinking and move into a new time of being responsible for all we create. Our thoughts become the physical realities of tomorrow. Without the thought of a wheel, no wheel could ever have manifested itself in this plane.

Maybe Angela and I accomplished nothing, but maybe we put thoughts of love, peace, truth, joy, and light into the world in a big way. I know that was our intent. And so it is.

In the Flow
By Winston

Early in January 1998 I had made plans to go to
Seattle to take a metaphysical class that would be offered
on Sunday afternoon. I also needed to find a number of
props, assorted colors of crepe hair for hair pieces, liquid
latex, and costume pieces that I needed for the plays I
was producing at the Trout Lake School, which would be
performed at the end of the month. My plan was to go
to Portland Saturday, shop for all this stuff and then
drive north to Seattle, spend the night in a motel, take
my class the next day, and return home Sunday evening.
It would be an easy trip in summer, but January is the
middle of winter for the Pacific Northwest.

By the middle of the week the weather forecasters
started predicting dire weather. An artic cold front was
moving down out of Canada and causing freezing rain in
the Columbia Gorge, and blowing snow into the Cascade passes. It didn't look like a good time to be traveling at all, let alone hitting all the weather hot spots. But
I needed those materials for my young actors to use in
rehearsal, I wanted to take my class, and I figured my
new four-wheel-drive pickup could go practically anyplace. I was determined to go. I looked forward to my
expedition.

On Saturday morning I left for Portland. The storm
was coming from north and east and it looked bad but I

was in front of it. I offered a request for protection and assistance in accomplishing all my tasks. I expected to spend at least three or four hours in Portland. My first stop was at a theatrical makeup supplier, where I found crepe hair in assorted colors, and liquid latex for building mustaches and beards. I also needed some bow ties, which I asked about at the make-up place. They directed me to a formal rental clothing place less than a mile away on the same street where I found more ties than I needed already bagged, ten for five dollars. What a bargain.

I drove to a variety store because I needed some toy pistols for a play written by the students in my drama class entitled "Late Night at the Convenience Store." I asked the clerk where I might find some realistic looking pistols for use in a play, and her response, after looking me over carefully, was that they were no longer being made, for all the obvious reasons. They did have some bargain-table toy police sets in the basement, which included badges and handcuffs, which I could use. The pistols in the sets, if painted appropriately, would function perfectly as Saturday night specials or police hideout guns. They had only two, exactly the number I needed. I had been amazingly lucky. I had accomplished all my shopping in little over an hour. It was starting to snow.

As I drove north across the bridge into Washington I listened to the weather news. It was not good. Snow and high wind was probably going to close I-84, the main arterial east of Portland. I could travel toward home on the Washington side of the Columbia, but I would still have the same weather. I decided to continue north up I- 5 to Seattle. Within ten miles the snowing and blowing ceased. I had good weather the rest of the way to Seattle.

As I drove I contemplated my experience in Portland. I had never felt so blessed. By petitioning or asking for help to accomplish my tasks in Portland, all had been possible. Why didn't I live my life that way all the time? Of course, I had a genuine need to acquire things that would enable my students to have a successful theatrical experience. I have always felt connected to higher guidance in my teaching, even when I don't ask for it. It just seems to happen.

I wanted to preserve this mood for the rest of the weekend. I found a motel on Aurora near Green Lake and planned to go jogging around the lake early Sunday morning. I was up before seven and running around the lake. The temperature was in the twenties, cold for Seattle. We had lived in an apartment two blocks from Green Lake for several years and I had enjoyed this same three-mile run then because there were so many things to see — ducks, geese, people and their dogs, and small boats. That morning was no exception. I felt wonderful and gave a smile or a "Good Morning" to the few joggers, walkers, and in-line skaters I met. I finished the run exhilarated.

The evening before I had called my voice teacher.
We had lost touch in the twenty years it had been since
I'd left Seattle. I had an appointment to go see her at
eleven. It was still early. I had plenty of time to go to
church in Bellevue where I had been the baritone soloist
and section leader for several years. As I drove across
Lake Washington, I relived the many times I had done
this in my former life as a singer. In my reverie I missed
one of the turns. Things had changed. There were more
houses, condos, and strip malls than I remembered. I
wasn't really lost. I knew where Saint Thomas should be.
I found it by driving around a bit.

I was filled with nostalgia the moment I entered.
Someone was playing the massive pipe organ that domi-
nates the whole end of the church, and the choir was
getting ready to start morning rehearsal. I walked up to
where the choir sat on both sides of the sanctuary and
saw an old friend. I walked up to say hello to Lucius,
and although both of us had aged, we immediately
recognized each other and hugged. He introduced me to
the choirmaster, explained that I had been a soloist there
for several years, and I was invited to join the rehearsal
and sing the first morning service. It was a wonderful
experience. The same feelings of being in the flow of the
universe that had been present the day before while shopping in Portland, and that morning during my run around
Green Lake, were even more pronounced as I sang and
enjoyed the camaraderie of the choir and congregation.

After the service we went to the adjoining reception hall and had coffee. Then it was time to drive back across the Lake Washington Bridge and see my former voice teacher, Mrs. Curtis-Verna.

Mrs. Verna and I had shared a teacher-student relationship for seven years. In exchange for extra private lessons I had done gardening, landscaping, painting, and other odd jobs on her beautiful home on Capital Hill. When one of her pet cats died, I made a small coffin and buried it on her place. In that time our relationship had become one of mutual friendship, respect, and love. We talked of former students that I had known and of our lives since I had left Seattle. I resolved to be better about keeping in touch. I left after twelve so I could go to my class, which was at one.

Most of what I heard in class was information I already knew. It all paled in comparison to the weekend I was having. The winter storm was still raging in the Pacific Northwest but it had missed Seattle completely. The Columbia Gorge was still closed and all the Cascade passes were under travel advisories. It looked as if the best route home was over Snoqualmie Pass on I-90 to Ellensburg, then I-82 to Yakima, then US-97 over Satus Pass to Goldendale and from there back to Trout Lake.

I listened to the weather news as I crossed back over Lake Washington for the last time. All passes were open but travel was not recommended. I stopped in Bellevue to get a full tank of gas, a precaution to spending the night in the vehicle. As I filled the tank I thought about the prudent thing to do, which would be to stay the night in a motel. I knew Trout Lake would have school regardless; they never closed for weather. I needed to be there Monday morning. Besides, I had asked God and the angels for help and assistance and received it. I needed to trust and have faith that this umbrella of protection would see me back home safe and sound. The adventure might not be over yet.

As I started up in the mountains I was impressed with the lack of traffic. I had the Interstate to myself. I had made many white-knuckled trips over Snoqualmie Pass in bad weather when I was younger and crazier. But tonight there were only a very few people on the road and no trucks, they were parked in the rest stops. It was snowing and I had tracks to follow. All I had to do was drive more slowly than usual.

As I drove I thought about the trip ahead. It would be nice to get to Reno's Pizza in Goldendale before their closing time for Sunday night. Reno's was a good place to stop with a bus full of kids on a trip; they always had wonderful pizza by the slice, a salad bar, homemade candies and ice cream, and fish-and-chips, my favorite. I wasn't going to hurry but it would be nice to get there in time. I was driving between thirty-five and forty-five miles and hour. It continued to snow as I headed up Satus Pass to Goldendale. Still, I was alone on the road. I arrived at Reno's Pizza with twenty minutes to spare. I knew I had been blessed as I ate my fish-and-chips. It was only fifty miles to home.

The highway outside of Goldendale had not been plowed and there were four inches of untracked snow. I had to watch the side markers to stay centered on the curvy road. I would be home by ten-thirty. I had called my wife from Reno's to let her know I was all right and would be home before eleven. About seven miles west of Goldendale, I passed a runner going the other way. Why was anyone out running after nine o'clock in the middle of nowhere on a Sunday night? I couldn't imagine that it was for physical fitness. The person was running too fast for physical fitness; he was not out for a jog.

I turned around and drove back toward town. In a short time I overtook the runner. I had to yell several times to get him to stop. I asked him what he was doing out here running in the middle of a snowy, Sunday night. He responded by telling me that he needed to go to the hospital; his mother was there. I asked him to get in. It was clear to me that I was there specifically to give this young man a ride the seven miles to the hospital. I had already been a recipient of a weekend of help, protection, and love. It was time to pay back.

As we drove to town I found out that the sixteen-year-old boy had been at a friend's house when he found out that his mother was in the hospital because of a drug overdose. He had no way to town except to walk or run, which he did immediately. We waited in the hospital for a time before he could see his mother. She was going to be all right, but she had to stay the night. I asked the boy where he was going to stay. He made a call and we waited until his girlfriend and her parents came to get him. It was now ten-thirty, the time I had intended to be home. I made another call to my wife and told her I would be home by midnight. The trip home was beautiful; my tracks were the only ones on the deserted highway.

I thought of my place in this grand scheme of things. How could I live my life more in tune with the workings of the universe? I didn't mind the uncertainty of not knowing, because I had just been shown that I wasn't in control anyway. I didn't mind being an instrument of assistance for other people. God helped me whenever I asked, and his plan for me seemed better than my own. Why not follow this path?

I didn't have to wait twenty-four hours for the question, "Why not follow this path?" to be challenged. After supper the next evening, Roberta, my wife of thirty years, said ominously, "We have to talk." I sat down and listened to her description of the weekend. She explained that she had been crying and talking on the phone the whole weekend and had come to the conclusion that we were not headed to the same place as we approached our retirement years. We didn't share many of the same interests beyond our work. The fact that we were both music teachers had always worked to our advantage, but she liked golf, bridge, and a social life, interests I didn't share. She said she had come to the final conclusion that she wanted a divorce. She was not comfortable with my spiritual quests. She wanted to spend the rest of her life with someone else.

I was in shock. It seemed fruitless to even try to salvage our marriage. What she said about our growing apart was true; somehow we no longer seemed to enjoy the same things. She had already presented me with her solution. I wasn't included. My whole life was about to change. All the material things I had acquired with Roberta would have to be divided and sold. I would have to make a new life for myself at age fifty-six. I spent most of the night in shock wondering what would happen. The bliss of the weekend completely disappeared. I had plays, performances, and teaching responsibilities coming up for the rest of the school year. It would be impossible for me to move, divide belongings, and prepare the house and property for sale until school was out. It would be the same for Roberta. We chose to stay in the house together until the end of the term. I received a lot of advice from well-meaning friends about how crazy it was for us to live in the house together, but habits of thirty years die hard.

Early in March I woke up to the fact that I was tired of living a "poor me" sort of life. I used the model of that special weekend to make a plan for my new life. I would update my placement file, find a new job, meet

new people, and establish new relationships. I could
have a brand new life, better than before. I just needed
to seek higher guidance and trust that I would be led to a
new and better life. I had been given the model at the
very end of my former life. It was still fresh in my mind.
I concluded that it had happened for that reason. I was
sustained by it as I found a new job in a new school,
made new friends, met my new wife, and looked forward
to the birth of Spencer, our son. I marvel at all that has
happened. I don't really know what will happen next,
but somehow I will be led to the greatest good if I merely
ask for help and guidance.

Last Good-byes
By Dolora

I walked into the nursing home my mom diligently went to everyday to sit with my father and hold his hand. Mom never wavered with her devotion. Not a day was missed from the time Dad entered the home until he left.

It was November of 1999 and Daddy greeted me with joy exclaiming, " DoDo, I've been waiting for you so long!" His mind didn't remember that it had only been two months since I had made the seven hundred-mile journey from Sun Valley, Idaho to Sandpoint.

Dad's physical condition had deteriorated. Once he had been a powerful man of two hundred plus pounds but now he was a frail being of one hundred twenty pounds who propelled himself down the hallways in his wheelchair.

My Dad had been a harsh and pretty judgmental person as I grew up. His basic drive was to earn an abundant living for all of us, which he did. His only version of play was to drive a speedboat across lake Pend O'reille, or fly the airplane that he loved. My Dad loved flying so much that he bought the plane before he ever learned how to fly. Now that's what I call confidence.

Expressing love was not something my Dad did easily as a young man, but somehow I knew he loved me greatly. As he sat in his wheelchair he somehow let go of all the barriers that his ego mind had once maintained, and he found that expressing his love was an easy thing to do.

I walked him to his room, fully aware that it was the last time I would see him alive. His swallow reflex no longer functioned, so he could not eat or drink.

I took him to the bathroom, helped him as you would a child, and then tucked him into bed. His legs could no longer straighten out, and he kept them in continual motion. At this moment in time his mind was totally present.

As I sat holding his hand he asked, "DoDo, what kind of a father have I been?"

I replied, "Dad, you have given me so many gifts as a parent. You gave me an incredible work ethic. You instilled in me a sense of confidence that told me it didn't matter if I failed, but it was vital for me to try. Your words were always "How do you know you can't do something if you haven't tried?" You always led me to believe every problem had a solution. You never showed me hopelessness. You always valued your family and made an effort to give us connection to all of our relations."

His next question was, "DoDo, what happens when you die?"

I replied, "Dad, everything I've ever read says you go through a tunnel and there's a beautiful light that draws you there. When you get to the end of the tunnel everybody you love that has gone on before will be waiting to welcome you."

Dad replied, "Wouldn't that be wonderful. Do you think that's the way it really is?"

"Yes, Dad, I do," I answered.

My mom and brother then entered the room. We held hands and remembered together all the loving adventures we had had as a family. What an opportunity to share all the joy in life a person has brought while they are still present enough to hear their praises sung.

Two months after this visit my Mom walked into my Dad's room and said, "Winston, you know these bodies of ours are getting really old, we should trade them in for a couple of new ones."

Dad sat up in bed for the first time in weeks and said, "You know, you're right."

That same night Daddy took the journey through the tunnel to the other side.

I will forever be grateful for the communication while his mind was still present, for we got to say good-bye in the most loving and positive way. It doesn't get better than that.

Until we meet again.

Gay
By Dolora

One of the blessings in my life is a woman named Gay. She truly is the epitome of her name although not in the sexual sense. Every morning when I walk into work she greets me cheerfully and gives me the most grounding hug you can experience. The energy flows from the top of my being all the way through every energy center until it runs into the earth and back up again. When you finish hugging and being hugged by Gay, you know you can overcome any obstacle or be in tune with any emotion and never get pulled off your center.

I have asked her if she feels the same when she hugs me and the reply is affirmative. The best description I can give to this amazing energy is a total balancing of vibration in each circuit of our bodies, leaving me centered, grounded and feeling loved beyond measure. What a way to start the day.

Gay truly is a gift from God. She has a degree as a veterinarian plus a Master's degree in counseling. She is loving, honest, and dependable, and above all she is my friend.

I had been asked to speak at the Celebration of Life for a mutual friend of Gay's and mine. Gay and her husband, another veterinarian, were in the process of moving to Hailey, Idaho, from Louisiana when we met.

A friend had arranged for the three of us to have lunch and discuss matters of the spiritual nature and get to know one another.

As I was getting ready for lunch my inner voice insisted that I asked Gay to be my kennel manager at work. I had been searching for three years to find the right person to be in charge of all the workers and boarding animals at our facility. Genuine love and compassion for people and animals was a necessity, along with an outgoing personality. Management and organizational skills would complete my picture of the perfect candidate. My intellect insisted that Gay was totally over-qualified for the position and we couldn't begin to pay her enough money to do the job.

All the way driving down to Hailey, a distance of about eleven miles, my heart and my head argued. Over-qualified my head declared. Ask her anyway, my heart would demand. Back and forth the battle went until I just said to my head, " Shut up." What did I have to lose? All she could do was say, No, this beautiful spiritual stranger I didn't even know.

I walked into the restaurant, greeted my friend and Gay. Before I even sat down, I blurted out, "What are you going to do when you move here? Are you looking for a job?"

"Well, yes," she answered, "as a matter of fact I am. But I don't want to work as a veterinarian and I have to be able to get away when my husband George needs me to do anesthesia for his equine surgeries."

"No problem," I answered. "Would you be interested in being my kennel manager?"

"Yes," Gay answered with a smile. "I really would."

I could hardly believe it. I had received a Yes. If I had listened to my head, I never would have asked Gay to work with the clinic. Now all I had to do was tell my boss what I had done. I went to work the next day and said, "Mark, I finally found us the perfect kennel manager. You have to take her to dinner and discuss the financial aspects of things." We both were overjoyed with our decision.

What I didn't know was that Gay and her husband had been receiving the local Idaho paper in Louisiana. The Wood River Valley is quite small, but due to the fact that it is a resort area, there are always lots of positions in the Help Wanted column. The only job that Gay had considered interesting was our position as a kennel manager. When I offered her the position, that was all the validation she needed to accept the job.

It has been a year now since Gay started working at the Sawtooth Animal Center. Her job has been very challenging in many aspects. Finding people who truly love animals and are willing to work as a team has required great effort. We now have a healthy team. We know the members will change as life moves for each of us. Laughter and trust are starting to manifest as we grow together in the business. Gratitude and love expresses the way I feel for having Gay in my life. Thank you, heart, for insisting that I listen.

Visions and Dreams

Visions and dreams can be glimpses into the future. The ones that come true can be recognized by a special feeling of peace, joy, or comfort. Winston

A Golden Vision
By Winston

In June 1987, Roberta and I flew to Boise, Idaho, and borrowed her parent's car so we could attend a round of teaching interviews in the Pacific Northwest. Roberta had explored the idea of teaching Music Education at the college level but jobs were scarce, she didn't quite have her PhD completed, and relocating in the Northwest would bring us closer to our respective families. We wanted to get back to four seasons, real mountains, and trees. We both had teaching credentials and experience in public school. Finding two public school music teaching jobs in the same locale was going to be a lot easier than finding two university teaching situations in music.

Our first interviews were in Medford, Oregon. I interviewed for a high school choral situation and Roberta interviewed for a junior high. We learned later that we probably would have both received a contract if I had interviewed at the junior high and Roberta at the high school. Roberta supposedly had an interview in the Olympia, Washington, area, but when we got there the staff wasn't able to meet with her. We had to get back to Boise to catch our flight back to Texas so we couldn't wait. From Olympia we chose to take the scenic route past Mt. Rainier and see some real mountains. We noticed that there was a secondary road that went from

Randle, Washington, to White Salmon, Washington. From there we could cross the Columbia River and take I-84 back to Boise.

We stopped in Randle and asked if the road to White Salmon was open yet. This road is closed in winter but by late June it had just opened. It was definitely scenic, slow, one lane in places and gravel for at least half the way, but it was beautiful. We drove up high on Mount Adams with snow on both sides of the road. The next town from Randle, Trout Lake, was such a beautiful sight for homesick Northwesterners. The Trout Lake Valley is picture-post-card perfect with the White Salmon River running through it to the Columbia River from glaciers on Mt. Adams. Orange California poppies bloomed in ever greater profusion on both sides of the already pictur-esque highway as we approached White Salmon. Just outside of White Salmon we stopped to admire the view. The sun was shining on the Columbia River from the west in late afternoon. The orchards below were laden with ripening fruit. The whole scene had a supernatural golden glow that made time seem to pause. Both of us felt the energy and beauty equally. We remarked about how special that place had seemed to be for both of us.

That golden vision sustained us for the next two years until we moved there in the fall of 1989. We came with no jobs, but we found situations immediately. I worked sawing on a landing for a logging firm, and Roberta found a job as a waitress at the White Salmon Elks club.

Within a year Roberta had a half-time teaching job at the White Salmon middle school and I was working in construction. This prophetic golden vision turned out to be a golden opportunity for us to advance professionally and financially. By 1991, we were both teaching and making plans to build a home someplace in the immediate area. We eventually found a beautiful twenty-acre place to build a home with a view of both Mount Adams and Mount Hood.

Finding a New Wife
By Winston

In early January of 1998, my wife of thirty years informed me that she didn't think we were headed to the same place in our retirement years. I understood that we had differences. I liked living in a remote area, puttering around our twenty acres, gardening, developing an irrigation system for our yard and trees, and having some animals to care for. She liked playing word games, bridge, and golf. Being with people and entertaining guests were much more to her liking than they were for me. I suspected that as we got older I would become more reclusive and she would become more social.

Being on divergent spiritual paths was also an issue; my beliefs were definitely closer to the fringe and less traditional than hers. My mother had broken away from the fundamentalist teachings of her mother because of restrictions against such things as dancing and theater. She raised both my sister and I to a much more liberal and tolerant lifestyle. My two nights a week playing in a small community orchestra and jazz band were social diversions that Roberta didn't share. I think my affair in Texas and my continuing friendship with Celia had been festering sores that were also contributing factors to our divorce.

The actual news, however, was devastating. I was busy teaching my regular schedule and producing two school plays. I spent hours at night wide-awake, staring at the ceiling wondering what to do with the rest of my life. For three months I merely put one foot in front of another and tried to meet all the requirements and obligations of my job and finish the season with the orchestra and jazz band. Roberta and I still shared the house. It was both cheaper and easier to finish our teaching obligations and put off dividing possessions of thirty years until school was out in June.

About three months after receiving the bad news, I decided to quit feeling sorry for myself. I started to develop a proactive approach by looking for a job that was: elsewhere, full-time, and more challenging. I knew that I probably would not remain single, but I was in no hurry to leap into the world of dating and emotional entanglements. I finished my employment responsibilities, Roberta and I divided our possessions, and by July I had accepted a full-time high school teaching job in Boardman, Oregon. I rented a one-bedroom apartment late in July and got ready to start my new life as a single man.

In mid-October my elderly parents, who were now living one hundred miles away in a senior citizen center in what had been nearby Hood River, Oregon, decided they would rather move back to Sandpoint, Idaho, where they still had friends. My father at eighty-six was getting senile. I didn't think my mother at eighty-three would be able to care for him much longer.

Early in November I came to Sandpoint, Idaho, to
check on my parents. I found my mother with bad
bruises on both forearms. Dad's equilibrium had gotten
worse. Mom would try to help him get up when he fell
but she didn't have the strength. My father still retained
an amazing amount of strength in his ham-like hands
and his trying to help mom help him by gripping her
forearms was causing the bruises. In addition, he was
more and more disoriented. My sister and I convinced
my mother against her protests that she could no longer
take care of Dad. We found a nice nearby full-care
nursing home where Mom could visit daily; it seemed
the best solution. I made plans to spend Thanksgiving
with Mom and Dad in Sandpoint.

With only two weeks until Thanksgiving, I gave some
thought to meeting some members of the opposite sex
and called a longtime friend of the family. Marilyn had
lived in Sandpoint for over twenty years, had lots of
social contacts, and probably knew a number of mature,
single women whom I might be interested in meeting
during the time I was there. I thought it would be nice
to see someone when I came to Sandpoint. I wasn't
looking for a permanent relationship. If I could go out
with someone for dinner, or a concert, or just for coffee,
it would add some interest to the bi-monthly trips to see
Mom and Dad. In the chance that something more
serious might develop, I gave Marilyn some guidelines:
mature, over forty, with or without children. I was

approaching the whole thing with some fear, and yet some excitement.

Marilyn had said earlier that she knew of several ladies who matched my requirements and might be interested. I called Marilyn after I arrived in Sandpoint on the Wednesday evening before Thanksgiving. She gave me the names of two women and their phone numbers. I made arrangements to take Susan out for coffee Friday morning and Carla for dinner Friday night. Not since college had I had two dates with two different women on the same day.

I had Thanksgiving dinner with Mom and Dad at the nursing home. It was a nice place for an institution; my father had good care. We spent several hours with him and then Mom and I came home. She still had some feelings of guilt precipitated by his not wanting her to leave each time she visited. Dad wasn't getting better and she wasn't getting younger or stronger. What had happened before would happen again if they tried to live together in their apartment. She could no longer take care of him.

The next morning I met Susan at Starbucks. I felt like I was sixteen. I found out that Susan had been through a divorce and had the care of her two children. Her life was full with being a single mom and taking care of her children. The coffee was good; I admired her for her pluck, but we didn't connect in any big way. I figured I would have to go out with her several times to get to know her better. I had already determined that I would not be intimidated by becoming a step-dad should that possibility occur; I work with children of all ages every day.

That evening I took Carla to Ivano's, a very nice Italian restaurant in Sandpoint. I found out that Carla was a nurse/administrator in a different wing of the same facility where my father stayed, and that she had never been married. She was such an effervescent, up-beat person that three hours had passed before I looked at my watch.

I awoke the next morning thinking about the previous evening and the fact that I had another whole day in Sandpoint before I had to go back to Boardman. I wanted to phone Carla. It was 9:00 AM so I decided to wait until ten. I didn't want to call her too soon and wake her on her day off.

At nine-fifteen the phone rang; it was Carla. She called to invite me out to dinner. She said she was concerned that I had spent quite a lot of money on our date and she wanted to reciprocate by taking me out. I explained that I didn't particularly need to go out to dinner again so soon; it would be more fun for me to just buy some food, rent a video, and let me cook for more than one. She agreed. We met in town, went shopping, rented a movie, and drove the twelve miles to her place. Our conversation picked up from where we left off the night before. After dinner we started the movie, but we didn't watch much of it. One thing led to another and romance started to bloom. We didn't sleep together. I went home about midnight, exhilarated.

The next morning I had a vision. I have had these several times. (See A Golden Vision and Direct Petition) I am awake; time seems to stop. They have always been intense and vivid, with deep personal significance. I had just awakened but was still in a sort of dream. I was in a hospital delivery room holding Carla in my arms from behind. She was delivering our baby. The baby was then put on her stomach face down. I didn't know whether the baby was a girl or a boy. I slowly came out of this vision in a state of awe. I asked myself, "Where did that come from?"

I translated the dream in my conscious mind. I had gone out with Carla with the idea that this would be a casual relationship. Either my subconscious, a higher power, or God had delivered a message telling me that this relationship had the potential to be much more than just casual. The message to me was that if I was not willing to accept the consequences of where this relationship was headed then I should walk away before reproductive intimacy occurred. Wow. I mulled this over and chose to keep this realization and dream to myself for a while. As I drove back to Boardman that day I thought about the pros and cons of being a first-time parent. Could I assume the huge responsibilities of a wife and child at my age of fifty-six? I liked Carla and wanted to know her better. Besides, a realization of the vision was probably only a remote possibility. Years before, I'd found out that I had a sperm count on the low side of average. The night before my dream Carla and I had done nothing to make any babies.

My ruminations while driving back to Boardman led me to the conclusion that I had nothing better to do with the rest of my life. I had already accepted that being a stepfather was a real possibility if I became serious about someone.

I had pep band performances for the following weekend, and Carla was not on call. I invited her to come to Boardman. Both her family and I were surprised; she came. We had a great weekend and I told her about the dream but not about its personal significance that our relationship was likely to become more than casual. I believe she dismissed it as a merely a dream. I filled the rest of the time until Christmas vacation with phone calls, letters, and preparations for school Christmas programs. Carla and I made plans to spend a lot of time together during Christmas vacation. We were married in the spring, and Spencer Howard Cook was born in the fall; I am doubly blessed beyond measure.

Carla and Spencer have enriched my life immeasurably. I had expected to drive around the country in an RV during my retirement years. Instead, I will be a husband to lovely Carla and father to this wonderful, smart, active, gift from God. This is a far better life for me than any I had envisioned.

Messages from Beyond

The communications received here, to me, are one of the greatest gifts I have been given on this spiritual path. Every instance brought a state of peace and joy to those involved. I am so grateful to be of service. Dolora

The veil that separates us from those who have passed on is sometimes thin. Winston

Rosamond
By Dolora

At the end of my freshman year in college, I became
very tired of the dating scene. The year was 1963, and I
was looking for a meaningful relationship. My parents
had asked that I work for them at their property on Lake
Pend O'reille for the summer. We were building a cabin,
or rather a second home, on ten acres of land located
right on the lakefront. It required a great deal of painting, insulating, tile laying, etc. My job was to help do
this work during the week. On the weekend, the lake,
95,000 acres of beautiful water, became alive with boat-
ers and families, all there to enjoy the fun of being in
Bottle Bay.

We had made friends with all the residents of Bottle
Bay and often six or seven families would come together
for a potluck dinner on Saturday night. Laughter always
filled the air. We took turns water skiing behind the
different boats and at night we would have a bonfire and
sit around talking and roasting marshmallows. In that
way we became one big, happy family.

Many of the families included young adults who were
all in college, and romance would often blossom. I met a
young man named Tom who was in dental school at the
University of Washington. We started dating during
vacations, seeing each other as often as possible all during
my freshman year at the University of Idaho. He was a

Phi Delt and I was a Pi Phi. At the end of my freshman year we became pinned. For those of you not familiar with the term, it is how people refer to the act of becoming engaged to be engaged.

His parent's cabin was just down the beach from ours. I loved his mom and enjoyed the rest of his family, but something was missing from the equation. I remained pinned to Tom for about nine months, but then we broke it off. However, I still loved his mother.

Several years passed, I was married with a fourteen-year-old daughter and an eleven-year-old son. I hadn't seen or talked to Tom in about twenty-two years. I had kept track of him through my parents, who received Christmas cards from him every year. He had become a dentist in the Seattle area and was married with two girls. I also knew his mom had passed away shortly after he had graduated from college.

One night I had a dream about Tom's mother, Rosamond. It was a lucid, vivid dream, and in it she asked me to call Tom and tell him how proud she was of him and how much she loved him. I was awakened instantly from the dream and I remembered it clearly. I also had no idea why, after twenty-two years, Rosamond would contact me.

Every time I would sit down to meditate, Rosamond's energy would be there asking me to call Tom. I would argue with her, telling her Tom would think I was crazy if I called after no contact for twenty-two years and say I had a message from his dead mother. Rosamond would not leave me alone, so one day I made the decision. I would call Tom's dental office and inform him of the message. It was a big step, to put myself on the line and take the chance of being considered unbalanced, but, oh well.

"Dr. Jones' office, how can I help you?" the office nurse answered.

"My name is Dolora, I am an old friend of Tom's. Is there any chance I could speak with him?" I asked.

The office nurse replied, "Just a moment, I'll check."

Tom picked up the phone and joyfully asked, "How are you?"

"Tom, I've had a message from your mom," I hesitantly stated.

Tom answered, "If she was ever going to come back and talk to someone, it would be you."

I took a deep breath. He didn't think I was crazy. "Tom, what's going on in your life?" I asked. "Your mom wanted me to tell you how much she loves you and how proud she is of you."

Tom answered, "Well, my wife just ran off with the man down the street and left me with two girls to raise."

I then understood the depth of Rosamond's love for her son. She had reached across dimensions to send a message of love to him at a time in his life when he needed it. I came to realize there is no such thing as death. Love exists and has the power to transcend all barriers. I was grateful for the communication from Rosamond and even more grateful for Tom's acceptance and validation of the message I was asked to deliver.

This experience taught me in a very real way that love has no boundaries, and it opened a door for more communication from the other side. I was ready to receive.

Just Listen
By Dolora

Bill was a physicist at the Trident submarine base in
Bangor, Washington, where he helped build torpedoes.
My husband and Bill and Bill's wife, Linda, had all gone
to college together at the University of Idaho. Linda was
a sorority sister of mine and by chance we found ourselves raising our children in the little town of Poulsbo,
Washington.

I had lost track of Linda after college. But when we
moved to Poulsbo for a new job I walked into church
and there was Linda. There are no accidents. She immediately introduced me to a whole new circle of people,
which was truly a gift as my children were very young
and I needed baby sitter lists, doctors and friends.

Ten years in Poulsbo went by. I had started a home-
based business designing leisure clothing and marketing
the garments by the home-party method. Many of the
parties were held across the sound in Seattle. One
evening I caught the 10:30 ferry from Seattle to
Winslow. I was tired and I went upstairs for a cup of hot
chocolate. Bill had also been on business in Seattle and
was returning home. We grabbed a padded booth and
conversation started. God wound up being the topic of
our conversation. Bill stated he didn't know if he believed in God, but he knew that there was energy. Energy, in his opinion, could not be created or destroyed, it

could only change phase.

I didn't think too much about the conversation then. It was just a way to pass the time on the ferry ride. Shortly thereafter, Bill was diagnosed with colon cancer. He went downhill pretty fast and passed away in his early forties.

About a year later we moved from Poulsbo to Sun Valley. One day, just about two years after Bill's death, while I was meditating, Bill's energy manifested itself. He asked me if I remembered the conversation we had had on the ferry that late night. I said that I did remember, and he then started to explain in detail to me how things work on the other side. Bill's reference points were all in torpedo terminology. He explained spirituality in terms of guidance and propulsion systems and tracking devices. Unfortunately none of this meant anything to me, and I told Bill, "This is all well and good, but I don't understand your information." I could see no reason to pass this information on to Linda. She had since remarried, and dragging up old pain did not seem to have a purpose.

I didn't think much about it until four years later when Bill popped into my meditation again and asked me to call Linda and tell her to back off, that she was hurting the children by trying to control their lives. He wanted to tell her to just love the children and let them take their journey. From my previous experience with Rosamund, I knew it was important to pass this message on. "Linda, hello, this is Dolora, how are you? I've just had a message from Bill." I explained. "How are the children?" I inquired.

Linda answered, "Maybe I should ask you how they are doing." Linda explained that her son was getting married and she and her new husband did not embrace the bride he had chosen.

It wasn't that they didn't like her, but she had a drinking problem. And, Linda was withholding her approval of the relationship, making her son miserable.

"Linda, Bill's message was for you to back off and just love the children," I said. "Let them take their own journey."

It had been six years since I had talked with Linda. She told me that the evening before I called, she and her husband had decided to let go of their criticisms and just be loving with her son and his fiancée.

Again, the message of love was so strong that it could reach across dimensions. Love transcends all barriers of time and death. When we send thoughts of love and peace to our loved ones who have crossed over, we enhance their lives as much as their messages sent to us on this side bring us peace and joy. When you get on the other side, the need to control things evaporates, and I believe that from that perspective our loved ones only try to help us.

I have committed myself to delivering those messages from the other side. It doesn't matter if my ego wants to protect itself. I have had to make it okay for people to think I am crazy. Not everyone can hear the messages, so I try to be a conduit for the love that comes through from the other side whenever I am asked.

"Everything is Just Fine Here, Sis"
By Winston

Roberta and I had purchased twenty acres in the
Trout Lake Valley in 1994 and we were contemplating a
number of different options in putting a house on the
property. After looking at literally hundreds of plans we
decided finally on a modular home with an open family/
dining area, which would embrace the magnificent views
of both Mt. Adams and Mt. Hood. The other reason to
choose a modular home was that it was both convention-
ally framed and capable of being lived in three months
from the date of our initial deposit. Having worked in
residential construction many summers while I was an
itinerant musician; I had the skills to build my own
home. I gave up that dream to have a house that was
totally finished inside and out by the end of May. I
would be plenty busy putting in water line, a quarter
mile of driveway, a septic system, and a regular foundation — all while teaching at the Trout Lake public
school.

At the beginning of April, Shelly, Roberta's father,
was diagnosed with inoperable abdominal cancer. He
had been operated on ten years before and again the
preceding fall. The cancer had come back with a vengeance. Shelly was given only months to live. We could
bring him to our new home in June and both of us
would be available to take care of him. Roberta's mother,

Buelah, who was getting senile, would have to be put into a home when Shelly could no longer take care of her. Thank God, we would have a place. The connection between Roberta and her father was very strong; it was logical that she would take care of her dad.

April and May were terribly stressful: Buelah would wander off and be brought home by the police; Shelly's health was declining weekly, we were putting in a septic system, foundation, driveway, waterline, making eight-hundred-mile round trips to Boise, and dealing with the spring quarter teaching responsibilities in Trout Lake and White Salmon. Our schools got out and we left for Boise the next day.

Shelly wanted to just stay at his place and die there. We felt we could do a better job of caring for him in our new place. Watching him leave the place he built, the tools and things he had loved his whole life, was one of the most poignant things I have witnessed. Shelly cried when his huge shop grinder was purchased at the sale we had. Shelly loved his things and he never threw anything away. He couldn't take them to our new place and he couldn't take them where he was going after that. I think that is why he cried. We moved Shelly into our new home and put Roberta's mother in a nursing home in Hood River, twenty-five miles away. Shelly was able to walk from the car into the house on June 15; a week later he had to use the wheelchair ramp I had just added to the back deck.

We connected with the local hospice chapter because neither of us were experienced care givers. They were wonderful to supply us with books, equipment, advice and on-site help. Their experience allowed them to prepare us for what was to come, including the emotional devastation that often surrounds such things as bathing and diapering a parent. My school superintendent, whose wife is a RN, also gave us help when needed.

Shelly had never indicated a belief in religion, God, or supernatural happenings. He had been accepted into the Masonic order, to which he was devoted, only because of a crafty argument. Shelly loved to garden and grow things. His Masonic advocate knew this and took a grain of wheat and asked him,

"Can you make one of these?"

Shelly answered, "No, but I can plant it and make it grow."

His advocate asked again, "Can you or anyone else you know make one of these and have it grow into a stalk of wheat?"

Shelly answered again, "No."

His advocate asked finally, "Can you accept that there is something greater than you that makes this possible?"

Shelly answered, "Yes."

His advocate told him that he obviously believed in a higher power and he was therefore accepted into their membership.

In the hospice literature we received, there was some

discussion of supernatural happenings that could occur in the last few weeks of a person's life. As the body shuts down there is little need for food and water. This stage can last for several weeks and it is surprising how well people at the end of their lives function on virtually nothing. Well-intentioned family members can cause stress by trying to force their loved ones to eat at this stage. By the middle of July, Shelly was eating and drinking practically nothing. He was concerned about what would happen when he died. Roberta and I, the hospice ministers and nurses all answered his questions based on our own respective faiths. It was difficult for Shelly to accept.

Either Roberta or I were at home at all times; it was our summer vacation and Shelly was never left alone. About a week before he died, I walked into his room to check on him. The room seemed charged, as if a large group of people were there. Shelly was sleeping but I felt uncomfortable being in his room. I saw nothing other than Shelly and I left quickly. When Roberta came home I said, "There were things going on in there," and she went immediately into Shelly's room. When she came out she had a quizzical expression on her face. She said that when she'd walked into his room Shelly was mumbling. He seemed to be talking to someone. She tried to talk to him but received only incoherent answers. Finally, he seemed to acknowledge her presence in the room. He looked at her and said, "Sis, there are players here you don't know."

Shelly died about a week later in the middle of the night.

Six months later to the day, in the middle of the night, Roberta was awakened by an especially vivid dream. In it Shelly told her, "Everything is just fine here, sis." The dream enabled Roberta to find closure concerning her father's death.

"Just Love Everything"
By Winston

Three weeks before my father's death in 1999, I was in Sandpoint, Idaho, to visit my future wife and help with the plans for my second marriage. Basketball season was over so I did not have to conduct the pep band for the games on weekends. My Oregon music job was on a four-day schedule rather than five so I had a three-day weekend. My father had been in the full-care facility for several months. His health was failing and it did not look like he would be able to attend the wedding that was scheduled for just two weeks away. I tried to spend some time with my dad every time I came to Idaho. He had days when he was fairly lucid but they were getting further apart. On this particular afternoon he was very concerned to tell me something. His speech was hoarse and very soft. It was difficult to understand him.

He motioned me to come closer. He grabbed my arms to pull me close to him. It was obviously extremely important to him that I hear what he said. His words, "Just love everything," although softly uttered, were spoken with total conviction. It took a lot of energy for him to deliver those words, and once he did he fell back in his chair, exhausted. We didn't discuss what he meant or why he felt I needed to hear it. My father never talked of spiritual things, or feelings and emotions. But this occasion was different. I sat quietly holding his hand, not talking.

That was the last lucid moment I spent with my father. I saw him again during spring break, just before our wedding. We saw him again before we went back to Oregon after our honeymoon in Waterton, B.C. He died three days later.

I look at this as the last and most important thing my father ever said to me. I recall it a lot, especially after a sharp comment to one of my misbehaving students, or when I am totally absorbed in something and ignore my son and wife. It is good advice. It is the umbrella I want to carry over my head all the time, but especially in bad weather. I try.

Roses for Emily
By Dolora

The year is not important, but I remember that the month was October somewhere in the late 90s. I was sitting in mediation, listening to the energies in my area of awareness. As I settled in to feel the peace, the centeredness of being one with all things, I felt an energy presence from my past that was asking to communicate. The energy was that of William, the Methodist minister who had performed the marriage ceremony at my wedding. William and his wife, Emily, had been good friends of my family in Bonners Ferry ever since I was a teenager in high school. On Sundays after church William, his wife, and their young daughter often came to our house for conversation and nourishment around the dinner table. William was a minister who was alive. He had a great sense of humor and he kept church from being boring. He had an infectious giggle that caused him to wiggle all over when he laughed.

I had not had much communication with William or his family as I grew older. I knew of their whereabouts through my parents. One day my mom called and said, "William dropped over dead with a heart attack in the grocery store." I couldn't believe the news. William was only in his sixties and much too young and vital to die, in my opinion. Emily, his true soul mate, was so devastated by his passing that her speech was adversely affected. She had had no time to prepare for his death and it seemed she'd been left without a reference point for reality.

My religious life no longer revolved around the Methodist Church, and I had not expected to receive any communication from William from the other side, but I have never had control over with whom or when communication would occur from the other side. When William came in to communicate a year or so after his death, I accepted his presence as natural and important. I asked him how I could help him. He responded, "Please send Emily a dozen yellow roses."

I said, "Damn, William, that's an expensive request, but I will do it."

I called my Mom and got Emily's address, I then did the florist thing and asked that a dozen yellow roses be delivered with a note to Emily saying, "William asked me to send these, Love Dolora." William and Emily were aware of some of my previous encounters from the other side, so this was not completely off-the-wall for Emily to experience.

I received a call from Emily expressing her gratitude for the flowers. Speech was still difficult for her so we did not talk long.

A year later I found out that their wedding anniversary was around the time I had sent the flowers, and that Emily had been at an incredible low point in her life. The roses and the message from William gave her a needed boost to continue living.

I had accepted long ago that if someone from the other side can gather the energy to come through, then there is an important purpose to communicate. Every time, without exception, I discovered that the message was important, and not just a figment of my imagination.

Quick Order Form

Telephone orders: Call 208-264-0176

e-mail orders: cook3@sandpoint.net

Postal orders:
attention: Winston Cook, WynLora Publishing
900 Trestle Creek Road
Hope, Idaho 83836

Please send me ____copies of
"Incidents Beyond Coincidence"

Name:_____

Address:_____

Ctiy:_____State___ZIP_____

Telephone:_____

e-mail address:_____

I would like a gift copy sent to :

Name:_____

Address:_____

City:_____State___Zip_____

Sales tax: Please add 6% for Idaho addresses
Normal book rate Shipping and Handling $3.00
Each additional $1.50